THE SAVIOUR

THE SAVIOUR

REV. DR. JOHN KENNEDY

Minister of the Gospel at Dingwall

Published by
Reformation Press
11 Churchill Drive
Stornoway
Isle of Lewis
PA87 2NP

Originally published as individual sermons in
Sermons by Rev. Dr. Kennedy, Dingwall
Inverness, 1885

Revised and reprinted with additional notes September 1992

British Library Cataloguing-in-Publication Data
Kennedy, John
Saviour. — 2Rev.ed.
I. Title   II. Dickie, Robert
232.9

ISBN 1 872556 03 5

Origination by
Settle Graphics
Settle, North Yorkshire

Printed by
The Craven Herald & Pioneer
Skipton, North Yorkshire

TO THE ONLY WISE GOD

OUR SAVIOUR, BE GLORY AND MAJESTY,

DOMINION AND POWER, BOTH NOW AND FOR EVER.

AMEN.

JUDE VERSE 25

Publisher's Preface

$\mathbf{D}$r. John Kennedy of Dingwall was one of the greatest of the Highland evangelical Ministers in the second half of the nineteenth century. There was "a galaxy of great evangelists, who were also good divines, in the Highlands of Scotland" during this period. Yet, even among these excellent men, the Minister of Dingwall was "the great preacher of his generation in Scotland. Dr. Kennedy was a truly great divine. The great Puritans had no more eminent successor in the Scottish ministry in the nineteenth century" (John Macleod, D.D., *Scottish Theology in relation to Church History since the Reformation,* pages 327-329: Knox Press, 1974).

What characterised the preaching of Dr. Kennedy? "In doctrine he was clear and powerful and at the same time practical. He was tender and judicious in his application of his message and he was an experimental divine in the best sense of the word. The preacher was a special master in the realm of delicate spiritual analysis" (John Macleod, op. cit., page 327). Under the blessing of God, "his ministry was . . . the means of enlightening, instructing, and encouraging the hearts of thousands of the followers of Christ" (Alexander Auld (Olrig), *Life of John Kennedy, D.D.,* page 96: T. Nelson and Sons, 1887).

The published sermons of Dr. Kennedy amply confirm these descriptions of the quality of his preaching. Almost all these discourses were delivered in the last two years of his life when his health was deteriorating. Some were taken down in shorthand as he preached. However, as his health failed to the point where he was unable to preach, he wrote sermons for his congregation.

"The written sermons would not compare with his preached ones. But the written discourses, set down with the deliberate judgment of his fine mind, give us the doctrine, practice and experience that the preacher meant to lay stress upon" (John Macleod, op. cit., page 327).

The Saviour is the first volume of a planned series of reprints of Dr. Kennedy's works. This book contains seven sermons, each one dealing with aspects of the person and work of Christ. The overall layout has been arranged to guide the reader through the development of each sermon. In particular, sub-headings have been added as an aid to the reader. Modern equivalents of obscure or obsolete words have been given in brackets. As conventions of grammar and punctuation have changed over the past century, it has been necessary to make minor changes to the text — this has been accomplished with minimum interference to the distinctive style of Dr. Kennedy's original. The Scripture quotations are from the Authorised (King James) Version: references have been supplied where appropriate.

The reader who prayerfully studies the sermons in *The Saviour* will readily agree with the assessments of Dr. Kennedy's preaching quoted above. This book is a rich devotional work, full of spiritual nourishment. It provides much material for meditation and prayer. The publisher hopes that *The Saviour* will be profitable to many under the blessing of God.

The Publisher   September 1992

Stornoway

Contents

Rev. Dr. John Kennedy

BIRTH AND UPBRINGING

John Kennedy was born in the Manse at Killearnan, Ross-shire, on 15th August 1819. He was the fourth son of Rev. John Kennedy (1772-1841), whose biography is recorded in *The Days of the Fathers in Ross-shire*. The young John Kennedy had the privilege of eminently godly parents, he heard the Gospel preached with unction from on high, and he was surrounded by those who truly feared the Lord. These circumstances left silent impressions on the growing boy; however, he remained in spiritual darkness.

EDUCATION

He received his early education at the local grammar school and attended Aberdeen University when he was about 17 years of age. He achieved several academic distinctions and easily obtained the degree of Master of Arts.

In 1840 John Kennedy entered the Divinity Hall of Aberdeen University. This was a solemn step for one who was unregenerate. He had a taste for light literature and one of his companions recorded that the fictions of Walter Scott occupied fully more of his time than the facts of John Calvin's *Institutes of the Christian Religion*. We may be sure that the father often prayed for his son, but it was not until the Minister of Killearnan died that these prayers were answered.

CONVERSION AND
EARLY SPIRITUAL EXPERIENCES

The death of his father in January 1841 led the young John Kennedy to seek the salvation of his soul. He went home to Killearnan for the funeral, overcome by grief. However, his sorrow caused him to pour out his soul to God. He subsequently related three particular aspects of this spiritual experience:

(a) Indescribable agony of mind under a sense of sin against God, especially in the neglect of the admonitions, instructions and example of his father, now lost to him for ever.

(b) Striving to keep himself from sinking into utter despair of God's mercy by betaking himself to prayer and to meditation on passages of Scripture.

(c) An apprehension that the way of salvation by Jesus Christ was opened in the Gospel to the very chief of sinners.

After his father's funeral, it was evident that John Kennedy was a man renewed by the grace of God. In the words of his biographer, "his former indifference to divine things had given place in his mind to deep seriousness, his self-sufficiency to self-abasement, the things of time to the things of eternity — old things had passed away, all things had become new". In reference to his father's death, John Kennedy could write: "The memory of that loss I can bear to recall, as I cherish the hope that his death was the means of uniting us in bonds that shall never be broken."

John Kennedy grew rapidly in grace and in the knowledge of God. He returned to the Divinity Hall in December 1841. Although he was not disposed to say much on the subject of the change of heart he had experienced, it was evident from his altered life, walk and conversion that he was a new creature in Christ Jesus. The Lord began to prepare him for future usefulness and for that place in the Church which he afterwards occupied as one of the ablest, most faithful and most highly honoured of His servants.

LICENSING AND ORDINATION

The nineteenth century saw the revival of evangelical religion in the Church of Scotland which had lain waste throughout the previous century. After a prolonged struggle between the Evangelical and "Moderate" parties, the

Disruption took place in May 1843. The Evangelical party left the Church of Scotland and thus the Free Church came into existence. The majority of the people in the Highlands of Scotland were well grounded in the scriptural principles underlying the Disruption and cast in their lot with the Free Church. John Kennedy was licensed to preach the Gospel by the Free Church Presbytery of Chanonry in 1843.

The newly formed Dingwall Free Church congregation required a Minister and their choice fell on the Rev. John Kennedy. He accepted the call and was inducted to the charge in February 1844.

MINISTER OF DINGWALL

To begin with, the congregation was small and poor. Yet it contained what was of far greater importance than numerical strength or riches — a number of eminently godly men and women, experienced Christians. What a privilege for the young Minister as he began his labours! Under the blessing of God, his labours were abundantly blessed to the edification of the Lord's people and he was used as an instrument in the conversion of many.

Dingwall was the immediate sphere of John Kennedy's labours. However, he soon became popular far beyond his immediate neighbourhood and occupied a place in the front rank of Scottish preachers. In 1873, the University of Aberdeen conferred the degree of Doctor of Divinity on him — a recognition of his many eminent services rendered to the cause of God.

In 1880, Dr. Kennedy developed the first symptoms of diabetes. Sadly, there was no treatment for this illness in the nineteenth century and his health deteriorated gradually over the succeeding years. He lost none of his vigour as a preacher or as a defender of Gospel truths and continued to preach even when he went to Italy in an attempt to regain some of his failing health. On the homeward journey, he fell ill in Edinburgh. He was unable to travel beyond Bridge of Allan, near Stirling, and died there on 28th April 1884. Of his death, one of his brother Ministers said, "At the news of Dr. Kennedy's death, the Highlands wept bitterly. The last day his face was seen on earth gave the most affecting testimony to the intense love and sorrow that followed him into the unseen. A stream of mourners passed slowly by the dead for many hours — the young bathed in tears, the old filled with awe as they gazed for the last time till the day of judgment on the face of one so greatly beloved." Thus closed the earthly course of John Kennedy, D.D.

DR. KENNEDY'S PERSONAL QUALITIES

Dr. Kennedy was a man of prayer, who realised the importance and solemnity of dealing with immortal souls. His ministry was valued by those who needed special spiritual help and guidance in their Christian course. He preached Christ with fullness and power. Some of his hearers were aware of their need of a saving change: many were indifferent to their spiritual interests. He addressed the consciences of the unconverted and unflinchingly presented the doctrines of the free offer of the Gospel and the sovereignty of God in the salvation of sinners.

In addition to his work as a preacher, Dr. Kennedy also became known as a faithful defender of the doctrines of the Bible in an age when the Scriptures were under attack, not only from an unbelieving world but also from enemies within the pale of the visible Church. Sad to say, much of the declension in doctrine and practice originated within the Free Church. Dr. Kennedy was one of the servants of Christ who were raised up to defend the doctrines of the Faith in those days of rampant infidelity.

According to his biographer: "There were preachers in the North who were as saintly in their character; there were some who equalled him in mental gifts, some who set forth the truth of God as fully and as faithfully, and some who laboured as zealously and successfully; but there was no one of these who exhibited such a combination of these ministerial qualifications as was found in Mr. Kennedy. His ministry met and satisfied, as fully as the ministry of mere man could well do, the various grades of character and the various phases of feeling in Gospel hearers."

[Extracted and adapted from *Life of John Kennedy, D.D.* by the Rev. Alexander Auld (Olrig) and *Memoirs of Dr. and Mrs. Kennedy* by the Rev. John Noble (Lairg) and the Rev. John Kennedy (Caticol) in *The Days of the Fathers in Ross-shire.*]

Thou shalt call His name Jesus

Thou shalt call his name Jesus:
for He shall save His people from their sins.

MATTHEW 1:21

Messiah was promised as the seed of Abraham, and as the Son and the Lord of David. The genealogy of Jesus of Nazareth given in this chapter is the proof of His being that promised One. Passing along the list of names, we find it divided into three sections — one from Abraham to David, a second from David to the captivity, and a third from the captivity to the birth in Bethlehem — to the coming of Him whose name is Jesus. Stopping, at the outset, beside Abraham, we have the light of inspired history in which to trace back his pedigree to the woman whose seed was to bruise the head of the serpent; and we can also look forward in clear light to David the King of Israel, in front of whose position is arising the brilliance of his son, in whose reign the summit of Israel's greatness and power was reached. Standing in that light and looking forward, the brightness is seen gradually departing till it passes under the dark shadow of the exile. Standing there again, light for a little shines upon the line which we are tracing; but again darkness supervenes, only to be dispelled when at last we come to the birth of Jesus Christ. By the light of His glory all other names are eclipsed. But if I feel as if out of sight of them all when I look on the infant in the manger, it is because they have helped me to recognise in Him the seed of the woman, the Son of Abraham, and the Son and Lord of David. It is sweet to find as we move along the line of genealogy that once and again a Gentile thread is woven into the cord of connection between Jesus and Abraham. To us Gentiles it is cheering to meet the names of Rahab and of Ruth — an earnest, even in these old times, of the fellowship of the outcasts with the peculiar people in the grace of the everlasting covenant. But how small seems our share in Him who was to come; yet it tells us that we Gentiles were never quite forgotten.

If we think of this chapter as a garden, there are in it not a few goodly trees; but whether they be cedar or cypress, apple tree or brier, they are intended to form an avenue through which to pass on to the Plant of Renown (Ezekiel 34:29), combining with the brilliance of the Rose of Sharon the pure beauty of the Lily of the Valley (Song 2:1) — and with the perfume of both, all the fruitfulness of the Tree of Life. O, that both I and you may be preserved from blindness, pride, unbelief and hardness of heart when now we approach the presence of Him, in view of whose birth the command was given, "Thou shalt call His name Jesus: for He shall save His people from their sins". The unction from the Holy One (1 John 2:20) alone can enable us to see His loveliness; only if we are humble will we come down to the valley where the fragrance of the Lily can be enjoyed, or sit under the shadow of the great Apple Tree. Only with a coarse hand can I touch the truth in which He is presented, unless spiritual life be in my faith — and only with a heart of flesh can I either seek, or trust, or love, or mourn for Him. Impressed with this, let us prayerfully approach the text.

To the Son, as the child born, a name is given (Isaiah 9:6). It is His Father's right to name Him. He has exercised His right. Before His birth the child's name is fixed upon. "Thou shalt call His name Jesus." And it is not without good reason He is so called. His name is to be according to His office. It is to explain the purpose of Him who sent Him — the purpose of the Father — and what His work, as sent, shall be, till at last the pleasure of Him who sent Him has fully prospered in His hands.

Let us then consider:

I. The name Jesus;

II. The reason for His name being Jesus.

I. THE NAME JESUS

"Thou shalt call His name Jesus." There is salvation in this name, and Jehovah is in it. A human child and salvation connected by a name of God's giving!

Jehovah and a human child connected! And so connected as that all that Jehovah is, and all the weakness of an infant born of a woman, subsist in the same person.

1. Salvation is in this name

This was in the first name of him who led the children of Israel through the Jordan into the land of promise. He was called Hoshea [Hebrew: Salvation] (Deuteronomy 32:44). He was so called before he acted the part of a deliverer to Israel. But in view of that work, "Moses called Oshea the son of Nun Jehoshua" (Numbers 13:16). The salvation of Israel must be associated with Jehovah, Israel's God. From Him alone it came, and to Him the praise of it must rise. But it is not only thus that Jehovah and salvation are associated in the name of Jesus. True, He is the Christ of God and, as such, God is His Head. And, therefore, through Him to God we must come, if we would reach the fountain of living waters; and through Him as Messiah we must send up our songs of praise to Him who sent Him, as to Him of whom and by whom, are all things. But I have Jehovah in the person of Him of whose office salvation is the design. If in faith I call Him "my Saviour", I may at the same time say to Him "my God"; and both I may say while looking on Him as He is, a weak infant in the manger — even though, as I see Him there, I cannot refrain from calling Him "my Brother". This is what this name represents Him to be.

Here then before us is the Word who was with God and was God (John 1:1), as made flesh and as bearing the name Jesus. What comes to you from God through this name? I answer: firstly, a representation of His glory; and secondly, an expression of His love. Jesus represents to us the name and love of God! It is as if God said, "This is My beloved Son, the brightness of My glory, and the express image of My person, and here He is in human nature to show forth My glory on the earth. And His name is Jesus. According to that name He is to glorify Me on the earth." Oh, is it come to this? Is the brightness of the Father's glory in human nature? Is He there that my nature may be the veil through which He is to cause the divine glory to appear? Is it in salvation He is to give forth the light of this glory? "Thou shalt call His name Jesus" is the answer. This is the Revealer's name. According to that name is the face from which the glory of Jehovah is to shine. According to that name must be the mode in which the name of God is to be manifested. His mind as to sin must appear, as well as His love to the sinner, and the glory of His wisdom shines forth in the arrangement which secures that both shall appear together. Divine glory shining from the face of Jesus is holy light, and yet it is the light of life (John 8:12).

17

It is as if He who sent Him said: "When Mine anointed One appears in the flesh — when He, who is My beloved Son, is a poor weak infant lying in a manger, in a stable, in front of an experience which will make Him a man of sorrows (Isaiah 53:3), and entering on a life which must close in the death of the cross — thou shalt call His name Jesus, that men may see how holy, righteous and true I am, when only thus do I fulfil the purpose of My love. Though His name tells how resolved I am to save, and how I commit Myself in all My resources to the fulfilment of My purpose to save, let men take knowledge of how My Son given as Jesus is both weak and poor as He enters on a life, and is to move on to a death of shame and sorrow, that they may know that My name is holy, and that My glory will I not give to another" (Isaiah 42:8).

2. The name Jesus shows the love of God to His people

"Thou shalt call His name Jesus, that He, according to that name, may show forth the love wherewith I love My people. Here is My Son as a weak infant in Bethlehem. The name which I give Him is Jesus. He is My salvation. He is the Saviour whom I have appointed to fulfil all the behests of My love. And He and I are one. Whatever love He expresses as the man of sorrows is My love. Let this name shine back on all the past till it illumines the portals of a past eternity and penetrates with its light the very council of the Godhead in which I set Him up from everlasting. Let it shine on the antecedents of My grace during earth's ages from the beginning, showing how I dealt with My people in days gone by. Let it shine onwards over the three-and-thirty years which intervene between the birth in Bethlehem and the death on Calvary. And let it in due time break forth, in its brightness, in the glorious Gospel, to be a light even to the Gentiles and, under its shining, look on all My ways of dealing with My peculiar people till, on a resurrection day, the work of their salvation shall be completed — and see and understand that I am love."

"Thou shalt call His name Jesus as He is now born of a woman. I have prepared a body for Him. I have not cast human nature (and all partakers of it) finally away from My favour. See human nature in the very person of My Son! Through that nature I manifest Myself. My Son's name who has it is Jesus. For through that body, when it is broken, I am to come forth with salvation." Fix your eye on Him! He is the door. Through Him Jehovah, as the God of all grace, shall appear. Through Him shall come forth the Spirit of Grace to fulfil on earth all the gracious purposes of God. O, those wondrous gleams of divine glory which shine on the river of the water of life, clear as crystal (Revelation 22:1) that comes forth through Him, as Jesus, bearing life to the dead! Thou

18

shalt call His name Jesus, and by that name learn both about the name and the grace of God.

"Thou shalt call His name Jesus, for so shall all sinners find Him who come through Him as the way to Me." True, He is Jehovah the Son, but He is also Jehovah the Saviour. He is the Son of man, who is come to seek and to save that which was lost (Luke 19:10).

II. THE REASON FOR HIS NAME BEING JESUS

"He shall save His people from their sins." Such is the reason given for His name being Jesus. This accounts for all that this name implies. If He saves His people from their sins, then He is Jehovah the Saviour. His great work is Saviour's work, and if He completes it He is, and must be, Jehovah.

The two questions now to be considered are:
1. Who are the people of Him whose name is Jesus?
2. What is Jesus to do for them?

1. Who are His people?

I answer: Not all whom He as Creator can claim as His. Not all over whom He is Lord; for just as surely as of one order of beings some shall be around the throne for ever and others in everlasting woe, so, if some of our race shall be for ever with Him in the Father's house, others shall be under everlasting punishment in outer darkness (Matthew 22:13).

Just as surely as we have here a definite purpose indicated, so we have at the same time a definite people on whom that purpose shall take full effect. Salvation from sins is the purpose because of which the Son of God was called Jesus. This was the reason why He was manifested in the flesh. That could not be before the view of Him who sent Him (nor before that of Him who came) except in connection with a people who were to be saved. It was no mere abstraction on which the love of God was set. The objects of that love were sinful men. And on these His love could not be fixed without His purposing to save them. That must be the behest, the determinate purpose of His love. And in the issue of an accomplished salvation, it shall perfectly appear who the loved ones were whom alone it was His purpose to save.

Therefore it is His people whom Jesus came to save. He came to save those who shall be saved. These were His as were none besides. They were His because the Father gave them to Him. "Thine they were, and Thou gavest

19

them Me," He says to His Father (John 17:6). He did not call Him to be His Shepherd without appointing Him a flock. He gave a flock to the Shepherd as surely as He gave a Shepherd to the flock — and the engagement of Jesus was to save from their sins all whom the Father gave to Him.

And just as surely as the Father gave them to Him when He entered into covenant with Him, so He promised to bring them unto Him in reward of His redeeming work, in order to their being saved by the power of His life. "All that the Father giveth Me shall come to Me," He says (John 6:37) in anticipation of the reward promised to Him by Him who sent Him. He speaks as if He were the Father's steward in relation to His people. For when He promises not to cast out any who come to Him, He does not base the assurance of this on His own love to the coming ones, but on His faithfulness to His Father. "For I came down from heaven, not to do Mine own will, but the will of Him that sent Me" (John 6:38). And He refers to the Father's will as the determining will, both in connection with the promise of the covenant and with the promise of the Gospel. Referring to the former, He says, "This is the Father's will which hath sent Me, that of all which He hath given Me I should lose nothing, but should raise it up again at the last day" (John 6:39). And referring to the latter, He says, "This is the will of Him that sent Me, that every one which seeth the Son, and believeth on Him, may have everlasting life: and I will raise him up at the last day" (John 6:40). His people, then, are those whom the Father gave to Him in covenant and whom He draws unto Him in the faith of the Gospel.

These, till the day of power comes, are just as all are by nature. There is no difference between them and others till the grace of God has made it. There is then a mark they bear which distinguishes them from all besides — they are a willing people (Psalm 110:3). They yield themselves up as sinners into the hands of Him whose name is Jesus, that He may save them from their sins. They yield themselves, too, as creatures into His hands, with all they are and have, that He may prepare them for His service and use them in His service. This they do unreservedly. They are free-will offerings unto the Lord.

Do you bear this mark? If so, you are one of Jesus' people, who shall be saved with an everlasting salvation (Isaiah 45:17). But if you bear no mark but one that brands you as a sinner — yea, even if you should be so branded as to be signalised as the very chief of sinners — as such you may come to Him whose work it is to save from sins. Till His name ceases to be Jesus and till His office ceases to be that of a Saviour from sins, and while you are invited as a sinner, you may come, counting on a welcome and expecting a salvation which shall be for ever.

Do any of you think that the view which has been presented of Jesus' people as an elect people is one that should be kept out of sight? Why do you think so? Is it because you think it tends to discourage souls? But why should it discourage any truly earnest seeker of Jesus? The fact of a doctrine being discouraging is no proof of its not being true. All truth is discouraging to false hope. And this doctrine is so just because it is true. It is, and must be so, to all who can tolerate no form of doctrine which requires an acknowledgment of the sovereignty of God and insists on the necessity of being born again. But to a truly anxious sinner, what is so encouraging as to be presented in Him — whose name is Jesus, who is Jehovah, the Son of man, and the Saviour — with a salvation that has all the steadfastness of the covenant, and all the freeness of the Gospel? What is so encouraging as to be told that grace is free, because it is sovereign, finding in the good pleasure of God the only reason of its exercise; and that it is only because of this that salvation is within his reach at all? What is so encouraging as to be told that the authority of the Sovereign Lord of all (at whose absolute disposal he is) is stamped on the call of the Gospel? — which is addressed to him, because addressed to all — inviting him, as he is, to come for salvation from all his sins to Him whose name is Jesus, and who has power to baptise him with the Holy Ghost.

Let none of you forget that, in dealing with the call of the Gospel, you have nought to do with the secret purpose of God, except in so far as it gives assurance of the certainty and grace of the Gospel salvation. You should realise that you are under the government of God. You should think of yourself, as a rational being, under obligation to do what He requires. You should fix your eye on the view of God's character revealed in the cross of Jesus. You should give ear to the voice of God calling you now, and as you are, to His Christ. You should be content with that as your warrant of faith. And coming, because called, you should commit your whole case into the hands of Him who, in your nature, is Jehovah, the Saviour from all sins.

2. What is Jesus to do for His people?

I answer: He shall save His people from their sins. By sins here are immediately presented to us their transgressions of the law of God. But these we must connect with their consequences and with their source, with the fruit which they produce and with the root from which they spring. The salvation of Jesus extends to all these. It meets the guilt, the misery and the corruption. It delivers from all to which sin exposes, and from all by which sin in transgression is produced.

He saves from the guilt, from the fruits and from the root of their sins.

(a) He saves from the guilt of their sins

Each one of all their sins made them liable to death. This must have been because of the curse of the law which they transgressed. This is the effect, friend, of every sin which you commit so long as you are without Christ. This is the force of the sins which you daily commit with the facility acquired by long habit. Little do you think of putting forth this awful power of self-destruction in sins which cost you neither thought nor conscious effort. You are a suicide in your times of deepest slumber, in the season of your greatest joy. Be easy or be troubled, be sad or be merry, by night or by day, in your closet and in the market place, or shop, or office or church, there comes forth from you a power that surely works for your destruction. Your lifework, Christless sinner, is to be heaping up "wrath against the day of wrath and revelation of the righteous judgment of God" (Romans 2:5). Thus employed were all the people whom Jesus claims as His, and who are His that He might save them.

Only as He appears in Bethlehem could He meet the case of such as these. He is in their nature. He is in their room. He is their kinsman Surety. He is in front of His great work in which He has by endurance of the curse to make an end of the sin which exposed to it, and by His obedience to secure a title to everlasting life. He must pay with His own blood the price of their ransom. He bought up His people. Not redemption for them — but themselves, that He might have a right to apply redemption to them by His Spirit. He bought with price that He might save by power.

And He puts forth His power to save in the mission [sending] of the Holy Ghost to convince them of sin, of righteousness and of judgment (John 16:8). Calling them effectually into His own fellowship, they become one with Him. He secures to them the imputation of His own righteousness and pleads on that ground for their being freely and fully and finally justified by God. His claim on their behalf conceded, they are delivered from all that exposed them to death. God has finally disposed of all their guilt. He has blotted it out — He has forgotten it — it shall no more rise in judgment against them. And the righteousness which merited this and the mercy which has afforded it both demand that they shall be declared by God to be entitled to everlasting life. Their sins are taken away, and in the righteousness of Jehovah Jesus they are set apart under the guardianship of God for the inheritance of everlasting life.

Friends, Jesus has this power of salvation. He has it now. He has the name which His Father gave Him just because it is His office (as it must be His delight) to exercise this power. And do not think that there is no concurrence of the Father and of the Holy Ghost in the gladness wherewith Jesus will deliver you thus if you come to Him. He cannot deny Himself — He cannot repudiate His name — He cannot cast aside His office — He cannot (for He will not) repress His love — He will not be unfaithful to Him who sent Him. Therefore He will in no wise cast you out if you come to Him for redemption through His blood, even the forgiveness of sins.

(b) He saves from all the fruits of their sin

This, in one view of it, is and must be implied in the removal of the guilt. But while all that is penal in the consequences of sin is disposed of in the cancelling of the guilt, there are results of sin which still remain. There is the trouble arising from its presence and power in the heart, the pain and unrest of the body, the active opposition and the hostile persecution arising from sin in the world, the trouble and grief resulting from the temptations of the wicked one. All these have some connection with sin. They are left to the forgiven people, not as part of their punishment, but as means of discipline. But when the time of discipline is over, just as partially during the course of it, His people shall be fully saved by Jesus from all these results of sin — from all pain because of a body of death within and a body of dust without; from all annoyance by the world; from all troubling by the wicked one; from all the unrest arising from desire unsatisfied; from all weariness of being outside the veil; from all the darkness that clouds the way through the wilderness; from all that would bar their entrance to the rest of the home awaiting them above.

(c) He saves from the roots of all their sins

These roots are in the old heart, which is declared to be "deceitful above all things, and desperately wicked" (Jeremiah 17:9). It is the work of Jesus to save from all these, by taking that heart away. But do not think that He is to do so all at once. Do not expect Him to take it away as He took the rib out of the side of Adam. He will not set you asleep, that His power may work apart from all effort and consciousness of yours. Don't expect Him to rid you of the sin that is in you by any conclusive action at the outset, such as separated your person and your guilt. If He saves from the corruption of sin, He will cause you to know what has to be mortified. You must be with Him as He, by His Word and Spirit, is searching out in your heart the roots of bitterness which have to be destroyed. In connection with each new discovery there will be a new sense of helplessness, a new application to atoning blood, a new cry for sanctifying grace, a new groan in connection with a new hope, a new conflict in order to a new victory in the strength of Jesus.

During all this process how frequent may be the poor soul's fears and faintings! How often may he be afraid that the good work has not been begun, and that Jesus is not pledged to save him! But Jesus is faithful and He is gracious. He preserves the life which He has begotten and keeps the needy waiting for His help against the power of sin. And however hidden meanwhile may be the glory of His power, however often one may feel as if quite forgotten and left to perish in his corruption, a time of succour shall yet come, in which a full end shall be made of the sin that polluted him all over and all through. The old man with all his members is, to his last moment, allowed to be and to operate within him, that the miracle of his extinction may close the life of faith that was started by the miracle of creation. O, poor soul, be not afraid, if you are willing to be rid of all sin and are looking to Jesus as your only resource, that you will be left unsaved. Or be not afraid that aught shall remain of your guilt, misery and corruption, which can bar your entrance into heaven or cast a shadow on the name of Jesus. Without perfect holiness His people would be shut out from the Father's house and the name of Jesus would be dishonoured. But this cannot be. He shall be glorified in His saints. His faithfulness to Him who sent Him requires that His people be without spot, or wrinkle, or any such thing (Ephesians 5:27), for the Father ordained them to be holy and sent His Son to make them so. His holiness demands this. If Jehovah is the Saviour, the people saved must be holy as He is holy (1 Peter 1:16). His love secures this. Will He not see to it that His loved ones are perfectly cured and cleansed?

PRACTICAL APPLICATION

I am now to ask each one of you, "What is Jesus to you? Is He your Saviour? Can you claim Him as your own? If not, is He the object of your desire? Are you content with Him as the only One who can save you from your sins? Do you feel pained at heart because of the power that works to keep you away from Him? Are you crying to God for an eye to see His beauty, for an ear to hear His voice, for a heart to accept Himself and His great salvation?" What is your answer to such questions as these?

1. There are some of you, I fear, to whom Jesus is not even a name representing Him who bears it — not even a word to the meaning of which you give any attention. It is but a sound which, unmoved, you allow to pass you by. O, friends, if you knew how indispensable He is to you, you could not be so

indifferent about Him. If you knew aught of His glory and of His grace, you could not thus despise Him. If you thought of how His Father delights in Him when He speaks to you regarding Him, you could not dare to insult His Son in presence of His glory. When I ask you today, "Are you to seek Jesus and His salvation?" your answer is "Never". That is your present resolution — or, at any rate, you have no other. You make no approach to resolve to seek Him — and under the power which sways you, that is just to let yourself float on the current that bears you away from Jesus on to everlasting death.

2. There are others who will not say "Never" when called to seek Jesus. They think they cannot be saved but by Him. And they know that if not saved they will be miserable for ever. They shrink from a final separation from Christ. But they are just as averse to open the door of their hearts to let Him in. While He stands at the door of their hearts they would fain that He remained outside till tomorrow came. But Jesus will not sit till He reaches the throne of your heart. There is no seat for a King but on a throne. While outside He stands ready to come in if the door is opened, but always ready too to go away when the appointed moment (known only to Himself) shall have arrived. It is a strange tomorrow this of yours, friend. It seems to be the morrow of every today you ever had. Many a today has gone, but this morrow of yours seems as far away as ever. It is today Jesus calls: the silence of death may be on the morrow. O, lie not abed with the sluggard crying for "a little sleep, a little slumber, a little folding of the hands to sleep" (Proverbs 6:10). You would fain have deep sleep which no anxiety would disturb. But there are times when conscience will not allow you to have it. Then you abate your cry. "A little slumber" is then your crave. You would at anyrate not allow yourself to be very anxious or let your fear obtain the mastery over you. But conscience presses you, and you cannot at all be easy. "A little folding of the hands to sleep" is your last crave, and it seems to you as if even of this only a little may be asked. You would hold your hands today from labouring for the meat which endureth to everlasting life — from seeking Jesus — but you expect to do so at some other time, when the season will be more convenient. How many act thus! What a brood of silly morrow-men that Felix has left behind him! Have done with this procrastination! Friends, today alone is yours. Now is the accepted time (2 Corinthians 6:2). Lose that and you lose Jesus — lose Jesus and you lose your soul.

3. There are some of you, when pressed to seek Jesus, who hesitate not to say that you have found Him. There is a yesterday to which you look back, as the time when you found salvation and peace. But what about today and your present feeling towards Christ? There is no trace of present brokenness of

heart. A sense of danger was somehow got rid of, and this is all you cared to have. A broken heart because of indwelling corruption, a lowly lying at the feet of Jesus, the needy's cry for help, the prayerful spirit and the weary walking — where are these? Alas! these are awanting. Friend, do not trust to a yesterday Jesus. Don't rest on any attainment of the past. You may have been deceived in your experience. Your peace may have been a false one — and it was, if you found it apart from Jehovah Jesus, the crucified and exalted Son of man, and if it was yours ere you were born again of God. Verily, deceived you are if not now poor and needy seeking the Jesus of today.

4. There are among you some who fain would see Jesus. You desire an anointed eye that can behold His beauty, a heart disposed kindly towards Him and a hand that can grasp Him in faith. To you, thus thirsting, the Lord will give drink. "I will pour water on Him that is thirsty" is His gracious promise (Isaiah 44:3). Would you have these desires satisfied rather than have all the world can give you? Then, friend, Jesus is yours. Your unwillingness to have Him was all that ever kept Him from you. You are now willing, you are now one of His people, and He shall save you from all your sins. Whatever be awanting to you, He can supply it. Whatever be your ailment, He has skill to cure it. Whatever be your sorrow, He is able to cheer you. Whatever be your weakness, He can give you strength. Whatever your unsteadiness, He can be the rock of your salvation. Whatever snares beset the narrow path of faith and duty, He can guide you safely through them all. Whatever your corruptions, He can make you clean. Whatever your trials, He can make them work together for your good. However many your foes, He can overcome them all. And however tedious your way and discouraged your heart because of it, He can bring you to the Father's house at last, where mansions await His people, in which they shall enjoy a home rest for ever.

Messiah's Beauty

*Thou art fairer than the
children of men.*

PSALM 45:2

These words are addressed to a "greater than Solomon". Solomon the son of David did not interpose, even as a type, between the Psalmist and Messiah, when he wrote and sang this psalm. Surely not, when he said to Him whose praise he sings, "Thy throne, O God, is for ever and ever" (Psalm 45:6), and no more can we think of an intervening type when he says, "Thou art fairer than the children of men". I am not to attempt to prove that this is a Messianic psalm. Enough, that it cannot possibly be regarded as true and applicable to any other; and that it is repeatedly quoted, as referring to Messiah, in the New Testament. I will enter into no argument with any man who is so blind as not to see Messiah's glory, as revealed in this song, and who does not regard as conclusive the Spirit's interpretation of the Word which He Himself had inspired.

The beauty of Christ is the matter of this song. "Thou art fairer than the children of men." How strange it seems at first sight that Messiah should be compared at all to the children of men! Must there not be something in common between them in order that they may be compared? Must they not in some way occupy the same level ere the one can be said to be fairer than the other? But is not Messiah the eternal Son of God? Is He not Jehovah whose throne, as God, is for ever and ever? Is He not therefore infinitely higher in rank and in beauty than any child of man can be? How then are they compared?

27

You must remember that Messiah is as truly the Son of man as He is the Son of man. He is a partaker of flesh and blood — true human nature. This places Him in a relation of brotherhood to "the seed of Abraham" and allows of a comparison between Him and them. It is Messiah, as incarnate, that is here before us; and it is in a believing contemplation of Him as such that the beauty referred to in the text can be appreciated and may be compared to that of the children of men. And in making the comparison, or in tracing its points, we must go along the line of His life and look on theirs as running parallel to it all the way from birth to resurrection and heaven. And if our eye has been touched by the unction from the Holy One (1 John 2:20), we shall see, step by step as we go on, enough to cause our hearts to sing in praise of Messiah, "Thou art fairer than the children of men".

Let us consider the following matters, in which the Messiah is thus fairer than the children of men:

I. The conception and birth of Messiah;
II. The growth of Messiah;
III. The consecration of Messiah to His public ministry;
IV. Messiah's service of obedience to His Father;
V. The suffering of Messiah;
VI. The death of Messiah.

I. THE CONCEPTION AND BIRTH OF MESSIAH

Let us think of Him in His conception and birth — for conceived and born He was. It was thus that He became "the Son of man". He was made of a woman (Galatians 4:4) according to the promise given in Eden. But His conception in the womb of the Virgin Mary was by the Holy Ghost. His human nature was therefore a holy thing (Luke 1:35) and was born without sin. The power of the Holy Ghost sufficed to secure this. The nature formed by Him was produced in union with the divine nature in the person of the Son, though quite distinct from it; and in it thus holy and thus subsisting dwelt the fulness of the Holy Ghost. How perfectly holy, how necessarily holy, how unchangeably holy must that nature be! How perfectly lovely, how ineffably glorious is He who appears as an infant in the stable of Bethlehem!

The children of men are conceived and born. But what is the conception and what is the birth of those who are descended from Adam by ordinary generation? Each one of these was shapen in iniquity and conceived in sin

(Psalm 51:5). The Spirit, as the Holy Ghost, did not put forth His power in their conception, although it was by God each one of them was fearfully and wonderfully made (Psalm 139:14). They were conceived and born in union with the first Adam, in whom they sinned; and as the result of their guilt, because they were chargeable with his sin, they were loathsomely corrupt in their earliest beginnings. They never were [i.e., had a being] without being both guilty and unclean. Those who are led by their own fancies rather than by the Word of God may speak of babies as "innocents". And parents in forgetfulness of what they are in the view of God and according to the Word of God, may idolatrously dote on their offspring as they look only on the beauty of their infants' faces. Perhaps, in so far as respects the only beauty which these can discern, the statement of the text might not be true. But when we think of loveliness such as God delights in, how true it is when we compare Messiah as the babe of Bethlehem with any infant ever born on the earth as a child of Adam, that He, in His conception and birth, is fairer than the children of men.

But if we compare His birth with the new birth of His people, still it is true that He is fairer than the children of men. Let there be no disparagement of the regenerating work of the Holy Ghost which precedes birth into the Kingdom of God. He implants what is a germ of all holiness. He produces a "new man" in a state of infancy, but complete as to all his parts, when He regenerates a soul. Perfect is that seed of God — but how much that is opposite to this is still within him who is born of God. There is a germ of all evil as well as a germ of all good — an "old man" as surely as a "new man" — within him. There is beauty in him, but how far from being perfect in beauty is he himself! Place Messiah beside all of the children of men who were born again of God, and it requires but little discernment to discover that He is fairer than these all.

II. THE GROWTH OF MESSIAH

Messiah is fairer in His growth than the children of men. In human life, birth is followed by growth in wisdom and in stature as one passes from infancy to youth, and from youth to manhood. Thus grow the children of men and thus grew Messiah. They and He may therefore be compared. But how fairer is He than they! They grow in wisdom as rational beings. Their mental faculties become stronger and more expert. But the wisdom in which they grow, what is it? Not heavenly wisdom — not wisdom unto salvation — only such as helps them to make use of opportunities for promoting their temporal interests and

29

for gratifying their sinful desires. In their case the growing wisdom is always under the sway of sin. And as they grow in wisdom, so they grow in stature. To the eyes of those that love them how interesting is that progress! Beautiful in infancy, some of these become fairer as they pass on to youth, and their progress is watched with delight by their friends. The infant has at last developed into full growth, and his manly beauty more than fulfils the promise of his earlier years. Yes, in all this there is much that is interesting and fair — but how few eyes outside of a narrow circle care to watch this development, and few hearts are disposed to rejoice in it. And how often, during that growth, do pains affect that body, the outcome in misery of the corruption which has made loathsome the soul within!

But what is the growth in wisdom and stature of any of all the children of men as compared with that of Jesus of Nazareth? (Luke 2:52).

1. Jesus increased in wisdom

But His wisdom was always perfect according to each successive stage of His life as the Son of man. Never at any time was there aught awanting to His reasonable soul. Each of His mental faculties was perfect according to the stage of His advance in life. And all His soul was perfectly holy, as well as perfectly powerful, in relation to all the activities proper to each season of His human life on earth. His wisdom was always perfect in its holiness. His growth in wisdom was no evidence of a previous defect. He was perfect as an infant, He was perfect as a youth, He was perfect as a man. The lily of the valleys was beautiful when a bud, and nothing was awanting to the germ of its more developed loveliness. Such was He who says of Himself, "I am the Rose of Sharon, and the Lily of the Valleys" (Song 2:1). He grew because He truly was "the man Christ Jesus". His growth does not indicate any defect — it but proves Him to be a true man, whom each one of the seed of Abraham may claim as his brother.

2. Jesus increased in stature

How wonderful it is that He, Jehovah, the everlasting Father (Isaiah 9:6) should be growing apace as a real man on the earth! There never was seen a wonder greater than this. But His human body never knew disease. All the more, because of this, was it sensitive to the pain of hunger and thirst and weariness, the pain of the thorns of the crown and of the nails of the cross, the pain of all the smiting and scourging inflicted by the cruel hands of ungodly men. But He grew notwithstanding all the enmity of the world and of hell, and of all the schemes which their hostility moved them to devise. Very early

Herod sought to slay Him, but even the King's power failed to accomplish his purpose. Yes, His growth in stature was wonderful, just because of how His life was attempted and his death desired.

His increasing stature was always moved by His increasing wisdom in all His bodily activities. The Holy Ghost, in all His fulness, was upon Him. And every advance in wisdom and in stature made by Jesus of Nazareth was always perfectly beautified with a holiness, whose lovely light leads back the eye of faith to the fountain of all divine holiness, in His own divine person, in the person of the Father, the brightness of whose glory He was (Hebrews 1:3), and in the person of the Holy Ghost by whom He was anointed.

3. Jesus increased in favour with God and man

Can it be wondered, then, that He grew in favour with God and man? How beautiful to the eye of God must His growth have been! He never could become more beautiful in the Father's view than He ever was in the glory of His holiness as the express image of His person (Hebrews 1:3), nor could He be more beloved as His eternal Son. But as He increased in wisdom and stature, He presented always perfect beauty to His Father's eye. He was step by step meeting apace His claims. And in His lowliness and obedience He was exhibiting a growing surety righteousness to Him who sent Him — in which, in His love to Himself, He delighted, because His name was being glorified; and in His love to His people He delighted, because they were being redeemed.

And as He grew in favour with God, so He grew in favour with man (Luke 2:52). Not with all men, but verily with all who knew Him as the Christ of God. None ever did grow in the true knowledge of Christ who did not grow in his esteem of Him. This was so when Jesus was in the flesh on earth; this is so now, and this shall be so to the end. This will be true of Messiah, believer, as He is in you — as it was true of Him, as He was in the flesh. He will increase in favour with you if He is in you the hope of glory (Colossians 1:27).

III. THE CONSECRATION OF MESSIAH TO HIS PUBLIC MINISTRY

Let us think of Him in connection with His consecration at His baptism to the work of His public ministry. Thinking of Him as He appears there, we may compare Him with some of the children whom God has called, qualified and set apart as His servants. But if we make this comparison fairly, we cannot refrain from saying of Him who was baptised at Jordan, "Thou art fairer than the children of men".

1. Messiah is fairer than the holiest of men

Let us compare the person, who is the man Christ Jesus, with any of the holiest and most devoted of the children of men. He is as truly man as is any one with whom we can compare Him. But His human nature subsists in the person of Jehovah, the eternal Son of God. How infinitely exalted therefore above all the children of men is He whose praise is sung in the text! And His human nature is perfect. But who are these children of men? They are of the lowest order of rational beings created by God. They are of a race which fell in the first man Adam; and to the meanness of their rank is added all the degradation of sin. As they are in themselves, that is the condition of all the children of men. They are men as surely as He is man; but they are mere men, and they are fallen men. How gloriously beautiful above them all is He to whom, though truly man, the Father's voice from heaven said, "Thou art My beloved Son, in whom I am well pleased" (Mark 1:11)!

2. Messiah's work was incomparably great

Let us think of the superior greatness of the work entrusted to Him. This was the greatest work which the divine purpose passed into the divine hand. It was so because of the vindication of the divine name proposed as one end of that work; because all the attributes of Jehovah were to be manifested as in the fulfilment of no other divine scheme — each one of them exhibited in this work in a measure exceeding that of all other revelations of it; and because on it depended the redemption of a multitude which no man can number (Revelation 7:9), all of whom were infinitely and eternally loved by God. And this work could not be carried on but in the face of the fierce opposition of the world and of hell. Nor could it be carried on except by one who could bear the wrath of God and live for ever after He had passed through an experience of that wrath being outpoured upon Him, and which could not be finished but in an accursed death on the cross. This was the work given Him to do.

But what is the work of these others, who have offered themselves as living sacrifices unto God? A work is given them to do; and it is verily great. It is so because it bears on the glory of God as its chief end, as well as on the spiritual welfare of sinful men. It is a formidable work in one aspect of it, for it is opposed by all the powers of evil; and each one engaged in it must pass from his service to render an account to God. But what is it as compared with the work which

32

the Father gave to His Son to do as Mediator? Nought done by them, in the strength of aught they have in themselves, can avail in the least for the fulfilment of the ends for which they are called to serve. But weak and resourceless as they are in themselves, the Lord can perfect His strength in their weakness, and to the praise of His grace secure that they shall serve to the praise of His glory.

3. The resources of Messiah

Think of Christ's equipment [resources] for His work, and then think of theirs. When we realise what He personally was and had, the perfection of His human nature, and the fulness of the Holy Ghost wherewith He was anointed, and then compare Him with His own servants, how infinitely He towers above them all! They in themselves have nothing but weakness; they have no resource apart from saving grace to fall back upon when faint before their work; and even the power to come for help they must receive as a gift of God. True, in the case of those whom the Lord effectually calls to the fellowship and service of His Son, there is a true hearty surrender of themselves to God — but this they owe to regenerating grace. True, also, they have infinite strength for the work given them to do — but it is a fulness of grace to be found in another, to whom they can only come as they are drawn. True, besides, the Lord has promised to be with them — but it is a gracious presence with them which they alone can expect. And though their labours may be fruitful, it is not by any might or power of theirs that this is secured. But in Christ is found all that is required as a perfect equipment for His great work; though as Mediator He honoured Him who sent Him by not using independently His resources — but instead of this, living by faith on Him of whom are all things and directing His cries to Him out of the felt weakness of the flesh, for help to bear Him on to the close of His work. But this acknowledgment of dependence only adds the beauty of meekness to all besides that makes Him, as the Father's servant, fairer than the children of men.

IV. MESSIAH'S SERVICE OF OBEDIENCE TO HIS FATHER

Think of Messiah as engaged in His service of obedience to Him who sent Him, and compare Him with any of the saints in their service. And if your eyes are not blind and the only heart within you is a heart of stone, how can you refrain from singing, "Thou art fairer than the children of men"?

When I think of Him obeying, there are two respects in which He appears to excel all besides.

1. The perfectness of Christ's obedience

In every motive and feeling and thought and utterance and action, Messiah was perfectly holy. He never failed, on any moment of all His service, to render to the law its claims in full. Perfectly conformed to it in His soul, all came perfectly holy from His soul into His work. The law could demand no more than He gave of obedience; and with every act of obedience God was well pleased. This was true of the whole course of His service. But of all other servants on the earth there was none who did not come short of the glory of God. Imperfect in their love, they could not be perfect in their obedience. They all must plead guilty of iniquity in holy things during all their service on the earth; and confessions of sin and supplications for mercy must be interspersed with all their work. O who, rightly comparing Him as a servant with them, can refrain from singing, "Thou art fairer than the children of men"?

2. The dignity of Christ's person

Jesus Christ is Jehovah, God over all, and yet He condescended to take the form of a servant. He alone, as servant, could magnify the law (Isaiah 42:21) under whose yoke He bowed. He — the Lord, the Lawgiver — obeyed! How infinitely wonderful this! And this was not inconsistent with His divine greatness. In the measure in which He is recognised as Jehovah is His right to absolute sovereignty discovered, and this is exercised in His humbling Himself and being obedient. And His human nature gives Him an opportunity of rendering the obedience in a way which consists with His divine supremacy, conduces to the praise of the glory of Him who sent Him, and secures the redemption of the objects of His love. He *might* obey, if such was His will; He *could* obey because He was the Son of man; and He *did* obey even unto death (Philippians 2:8). How much fairer was He than those who were but men and sinful! They could neither fulfil nor honour the law. They were honoured by being required to obey. They got honour by being called to serve; they could not give honour by their service. O how sweet it is to discover His excellence as the servant who was one with Him who sent Him! Men speak of feasting their eyes on beauty — but here is beauty on which you can feast your heart! And as it yields a feast to all lovers of Christ, it is healing to the wounds of the diseased — a balm which never fails to cure.

V. THE SUFFERING OF MESSIAH

Think of His beauty as it appears in His suffering, and compare Him with all the children of men who pass through great tribulation into the Kingdom. He was a sin-bearer, and yet He was sinless in all His sufferings. He was made sin (2 Corinthians 5:21) by the imputation to Him of the sins of the people for whom He undertook to act the part of Surety, so that towards Him came forth a full expression of the wrath of God because of sin. Thus, and thus alone, can His suffering be accounted for.

And all throughout His suffering He was expressing His love to the sinful people whom He represented. Every reproach He bore, every sigh He heaved, every pain He endured, all His hunger and thirst and weariness, all His agony of soul — all was for them. And He knew it was for them — and knew how utterly unworthy they were — and yet He not only bore with meekness all He suffered in their behalf, but was eager to drink the bitter cup which was filled with their deserts that not one drop should have to be tasted by them.

It was Emmanuel who suffered as the Surety because He was the lover of His people. O what a sight is before us, in such a One being in the midst of penal suffering that could terminate only in His death! O, this is the wonder of wonders! Because Divine justice was first feasted by the sufferings of the divine Redeemer, it can be a feast for me! O, what was rendered, as a ransom, in sufferings such as His! Divine blood shed to make atonement for sin! On each moment of the suffering of such a One, as He who was "the Word made flesh", there came what was of infinite value into the treasury of heaven — and what was implied in all which He endured, what mind but God's own can comprehend? But it sufficed. "Mercy and truth are met together; righteousness and peace have kissed each other" (Psalm 85:10).

Compare this glorious and gracious sufferer with all suffering children of men, and how true it will appear that He is fairer than any of them all! What is the suffering of such of these as are in a state of nature, except a small measure of what is due to them as sinners? — while during the whole course of their suffering they are acting towards God, according to the enmity of their carnal minds, and deriving no benefit themselves, they secure no benefit to others by all that they endure. Surely, then, when we look on the sinless One, who suffered for others that they might be redeemed, and who is Emmanuel, how can we refrain from singing, "Thou art fairer than the children of men"?

But He is fairer even than those children of men who are suffering for His sake. There is some beauty to be seen in them. They love the Lord Jesus, and that is the greatest beauty they present. True, they are clothed with His righteousness, and thus it may be said that there was perfect beauty put upon them; but all this must be ascribed to Him who wrought out this righteousness for them at the cost of dying. The beauty in them is the measure of their love to Messiah — and this is but imperfect in the holiest of them all. How much besides this love breaks out in and from their hearts when they are passing through the fire of affliction! And there is no vicariousness in their sufferings. Much of it arises from their own sin, because of which the Lord must chasten them. And they can secure neither to themselves nor to others any benefit from all that they endure. And what are they but mere men — mean worms of the dust — in comparison with the high and lofty One who inhabiteth eternity? True, there is beauty in the meekness and constancy which by the help of grace they exhibit in the midst of their troubles. But what is this as compared with the meekness of the Lamb of God and with the constancy of Him who said, "I set my face like a flint, and I know that I shall not be ashamed"? Thus, though all children of men who are graceless suffer — and many of them suffer much; and though all who enter the Kingdom of God pass through great tribulation — as they pass through the fire to the glory which is soon to be revealed (Romans 8:18) these exhibit the beauty of meekness and of constancy — yet Messiah, as compared with these all, is such that every one who has seen His beauty must heartily sing, "Thou art fairer than the children of men"!

VI. THE DEATH OF MESSIAH

Messiah died, and the children of men shall die — but the eye that beholds Him in His dying must discover that in His death, as compared with theirs, He is fairer than them all. His death is the perfect closing act of His obedience to Him who sent Him. It is the crowning expression of His love to His guilty people. It gives its finish to the work of redemption. It seals the everlasting covenant and secures all its blessings to those for whom He, by His blood, paid the ransom price. And His death on the tree completed His expression of love to the Father who sent Him, and to the people whom He charged Him to redeem. Connecting His death with the glory of His divine person, how sin is seen to be made an end of by the curse being exhausted — and thus is justice satisfied, the law magnified, and the name of God glorified. O what a sweet savour of meekness, love and merit issues from the cross on which Jesus poured out

His soul unto death (Isaiah 53:12)! O the ineffable loveliness of the Son of God, as the Lamb of God, hanging dead on the accursed tree!

Surely it is not difficult to know Him, as He is there and thus before us, as being fairer than the children of men who die unsaved. *On* them is all the guilt of their iniquity, *over* them is all the fearfulness of the curse, and *in* them is a fulness of corruption that ripens them for hell. He died an accursed death, and so do they; and this allows of a comparison between them. His death effected a separation between His soul and His body; and thus, too, death severs them in twain; and as He was buried, so are they. But if on these accounts we may compare Him with them, how ineffably great is the difference in His favour, because of which the song of the text must be sung to His praise! He is a divine person; they are mere men. He was holy, harmless, undefiled, separate from sinners; and they are loathsome criminals. He died because the sins of others were laid upon Him; they die because their own sins remain upon them. He triumphs over death as the Prince of life; they are death's captives, and it triumphs in their destruction. He passed through death to the midst of the throne of God; they pass through it into the fire that never shall be quenched. O yes, glorious Messiah, "Thou," in Thy dying, "art fairer than the children of men"!

And still may this song be sung to His praise, when we place Him beside all children of men who die in the Lord. What beauty do they present, except what they owe to Him? Their comeliness has been put upon them. And if, as they have passed through death, they are all glorious within, it is He who made them so. Any light that shines from them, out of the darkness of death, is the reflection of what shone upon and into them from Him, as the light of the world (John 8:12). They bring, in their hearts, the seed of all corruption, up to the very moment of their dying; while He in living and dying knew no sin (2 Corinthians 5:21). They pass through death to heaven, to occupy a mansion prepared for those who shall serve for ever; while He, as the glorious Head, passed through death, to be, in human nature, in His place as the eternal Son of God, reigning there till all His enemies are subdued, all His loved ones saved, and till the pleasure of the Lord hath fully prospered in His hand (Isaiah 53:10). Fair in His death, exceedingly beyond all the children of men, is Messiah whose praise is sung in the text.

Thus, whether we compare Messiah, as the Son of man, in His birth, or in His growth, or in His consecration, or in His obedience, or in His suffering, or in His death, with any of the children of men, fairer than the fairest of them is He in His matchless beauty! O for faces unveiled! that we may behold as in a glass the glory of the Lord and thus be changed into the same image, from glory to glory, even as by the Spirit of the Lord (2 Corinthians 3:18).

PRACTICAL APPLICATION

I would ask each one of you a question — to which you should desire to give an honest answer, as in the presence of God. The question is, "Have you ever so seen the beauty of Christ, that your heart was sweetly constrained to utter, as a song in His praise, the words of the text?". What is your answer to this question?

1. One says, "I hope I have thus known and praised Him, but dim was my view of His beauty and short-lived was my song in His praise". But if there was one moment of a true appreciation of Christ, however unworthy you deemed it, and one moment of true praise evoked by His beauty, what a debtor you are to God for the eye to see and for the heart to praise! Unless He had quickened you and revealed His Son in you, you would not have the desire to know and trust and love Him, which is like a painful, unsatisfied thirst within you. And it is only by being a willing debtor still to God that you can possibly attain to further soul-transforming views of Messiah. Ask this of Him who giveth liberally and upbraideth not, and it shall be given you (James 1:5). And do not postpone your thanksgiving till you attain to sing in praise of Messiah as you would fain desire to sing it. If you do so, you will never render a thank-offering to God till you enter heaven. But there is music to the ear of God in the broken thanksgiving that comes from true hearts on the earth, as surely as in the perfect praise of heaven. Thanksgivings on earth there should be for all grace-givings on earth.

2. Another says, "I wish I could praise Him. I cannot say that my heart has ever been truly disposed to prize or praise Him and I fear, because of my darkness and deadness, that I shall remain blind and dumb to the end." But why does your want of a heart to praise the Lord grieve you? Surely if you had no love to Him you would not care to praise Him. And why should you despair because you cannot open your own eyes nor soften your own heart? This is not work for you to attempt. This is the work of Messiah Jesus, and He has the heart and the hand for such a work. In a moment He could shine away your darkness, and stir up your heart to sing. Let your chosen place be at His feet. Tell Him of the blind eyes and of the dumb heart; and however long He may delay in effecting a cure, verily He will not allow you to perish in the dark.

3. Another still says, "I never praised Him, and it is very unlikely that I ever will". Do not imagine that you must always speak truly when you speak hopelessly. And yet you are very prone to think this. Your old covenant spirit and your unbelief combine to make you disposed to entertain such an idea. When you find in yourself only what makes you feel quite dependent on the grace of God, you lose heart, as if there were no other resource; and your unbelief takes advantage of your experience of the presence and power of sin to prophesy shame to you as your portion in the future. But are you sure, on good grounds, of your never having (in your heart's desire) praised the Lord in days past? If you had any thirst for praising grace, then there was grace praising in the desire to praise. And if you know to whom to go in your helplessness, though you cannot say that you ever reached Him, wait for His coming to your help — only let there be watching in your waiting. Let it be the waiting of one who cannot sleep till help comes; not like that of the sluggard whose soul "desireth and hath nothing" (Proverbs 13:4). And who told you that you never would be visited by the salvation of the Lord? The Lord has not told you so; therefore it cannot be a thing to be believed. If you have told it to yourself, what is that but a deceiver cheating a fool? If Satan tells it, then surely you would be utterly mad if you allowed yourself to be influenced by him who was a liar and a murderer from the beginning (John 8:44). If you cannot tell whence the suggestion comes, then there is nothing to make it worthy of consideration, and you should just sweep it into the rubbish heap. Hear the voice of Messiah, the Son of man calling to the simple ones and saying, "Turn you at My reproof: behold I will pour out My Spirit unto you, I will make known My words unto you" (Proverbs 1:22-23).

4. Another answers, "I cannot say that I have thought seriously yet of how I am affected towards Messiah, or Messiah towards me; but when I have a more convenient season I will take up the question". And what more important question can you take up? There is none whatever; and yet you are giving all you have of time to the trifles and leaving the one thing needful outside your care. Can you dare to say that, even in your own eyes, this seems to be right? And is tomorrow yours, so that you can reckon on "a more convenient season"? Why, friend, you never have as yours but the present moment. On the next your soul may be passing into eternity. And even if you might reckon on many years being before you, is it likely that a more convenient season than the present can come? What makes a season convenient? Is it not that it brings to you an opportunity of escape from the wrath to come? And what is required in order to your benefiting by having that opportunity? Is it not the Lord's

coming to make it a day of power (Psalm 110:3) and a time of love (Ezekiel 16:8)? And have you God at your command, so that you may reckon on His acting thus? Friend, you may not expect help from Him except while He is calling you. You cannot warrantably ask God to come to visit you except *now* while He is calling to you. Friend, your procrastination arises from your dislike earnestly to deal with God. And do you think that by continuing to engross yourself with the trifling things of the world, and by leaving yourself under the power of sin and Satan, you will become more disposed to use the opportunity which the Gospel affords? No, verily! In following Felix (Acts 24:24-25) you follow one who was both a dupe and a deceiver.

5. Another replies, "I have not troubled myself with these things, and I do not purpose to do so". He who gives this reply speaks for a great many, who so allow the world to engross them that they never at all allow themselves to think of Messiah. He is not in all their thoughts. And instead of thinking of themselves as fools, they are disposed to reckon all to be so who differ from themselves. But the most foolish of all simpletons are these! For what is their choice? Is it that which is of real and enduring value? Or is it that which cannot profit and cannot last? The latter is the object of their choice. And yet they call themselves wise! And they think of sinning against Christ as a very venial offence. At least they themselves can easily pardon it — and for divine pardon they care not. And why does it appear so to them? It is because He against whom they sin is utterly unknown and heartily hated. To despise Him — to act as if He were not — they reckon to be no offence at all. Therefore they have no fear in prospect of the future. But thus says Messiah, He whom these despise, "Because I have called, and ye refused; I have stretched out my hand, and no man regarded; but ye have set at nought all my counsel, and would none of my reproof: I also will laugh at your calamity; I will mock when your fear cometh" (Proverbs 1:24-26). For while the day of vengeance is coming, their fear is coming with it — the vengeance to overwhelm them, and the fear to make their heart, so long cold and callous, to tremble to its core.

Yes, the day of vengeance, which shall be a day of tribulation, shall soon overtake all the enemies of the Messiah, for thus saith the Lord, "If any man love not the Lord Jesus Christ, let him be Anathema Maranatha" (1 Corinthians 16:22) — let the curse of God take effect upon him at the coming of the Lord to judgment. Can we wonder that it should be so? How possibly, under the government of God, could they who love not the Lord Jesus Christ escape this righteous judgment? He whom they would not love was the Lord, the divine One, who in human nature is now exalted as Lord to His place in the midst of the throne of God. Divine glory is now shining forth from Him on the throne of God through the veil of human nature! And yet He is not loved! And He to whom this place of power and glory belongs, though claiming homage, received only angry contempt. And can they who thus dishonoured His Son escape the righteous judgment of God? He whom they refuse to love is Jesus, the Saviour of sinners, the gracious and omnipotent Saviour, the divine person, who became a weak babe in Bethlehem, who lived the life of a man of sorrows, and died on the cross because made both sin and a curse for those who were His enemies, and who is ready to act according to this sweet name towards all who come to Him — even towards the very guiltiest of all. And He who was despised is Messiah, who was faithful to Him who sent Him, in finishing the work given to Him to do, and in whose hand the Father's pleasure is, that the power of His life might cause it to prosper in the salvation of all whom He redeemed by the work which He finished on the cross.

O think, if only for a moment, of what not loving such a One implies! Think of His divine and mediatorial glory as the Lord! Think of His love to sinners expressed in the sorrow of His life and in the shame and agony of His death! Think of how He obeyed and suffered according to the Father's will, and of how He now has in His hand the Father's pleasure! Think of how He is regarded in heaven, commended in the Gospel and loved by His people, who chose to die rather than to forsake Him! And then try to excuse yourself, if you can, for not loving Him. I know you will attempt to excuse your want of love to Messiah, but your excuse is such as can satisfy only a fool — that fool being yourself. But, in the view of God, nothing short of destruction from the presence of the Lord can requite the sin of their not loving Him of whom He said, "This is my beloved Son in whom I am well pleased" (Matthew 3:17). And it is through Messiah Himself the wrath is to be expressed which shall be as devouring fire to all who loved Him not. How awful is divine judgment thus taking effect! How it must tell in the extinction of all hope in the hearts of all on whom it comes! All Messiah's enemies shall be made His footstool, that His power may for ever crush them. Beware, lest you be for ever one of these!

Christ's Love to the Church

Christ also loved the Church and gave Himself for it;
that He might sanctify and cleanse it with the washing of water by the Word,
that He might present it to Himself a glorious Church, not having
spot, or wrinkle, or any such thing; but that it should be
holy and without blemish.

EPHESIANS 5:25-27

In the first statement of this text Christ and the Church are seen linked together, the connecting link being love, and the love being Christ's — "Christ also loved the Church". In the second statement we have the great expression of His love in its behalf — He "gave Himself for it". In the third statement we are shown the outflow of His love to the Church in washing and sanctifying grace — "that He might sanctify and cleanse it with the washing of water by the Word". And in the remaining portion of the text, there is exhibited to us the ripe fruit of Christ's love, in the final condition of the Church — "that He might present it to Himself a glorious Church, not having spot, or wrinkle, or any such thing; but that it should be holy and without blemish".

In speaking, therefore, from this text, these are the four things to which we are to call your attention:

    I. Christ's love to the Church;

   II. Christ gave Himself for the Church;

 III. The outflowing of Christ's love;

 IV. The ripe fruit of Christ's love.

These four things are indissolubly linked together. This is done by God. And what, therefore, God has joined together, let no man put asunder. If Christ loved the Church, it was because such was His sovereign will. But having loved it, the expression of that love in His giving Himself for it seems to be necessary. We cannot ascribe to such love as His an aimless unsuitable display — a mere ineffective demonstration. The case of the loved one must be exactly and effectively met by such a lover. And once this display of His love has been given, it must tell on the object of love. Such a sacrifice in its behalf must tell on the condition of the Church — the Church for which He gave Himself must be cleansed and sanctified. And such love as has been displayed in an atonement in its behalf — and has affected it, as cleansing and sanctifying grace — must secure finally and for ever the perfect purity and blessedness of the Church because of these aspects of love — its bounty, its unchangeableness, its resources, its costly antecedent, its pledges and its holiness. The love of Christ, being the infinite love of God, cannot be fruitless; and once I believe that Christ loved, then I cannot but be assured that all ascribed to His love in the text shall infallibly flow from it, as priceless benefit to all who are its objects.

I. CHRIST'S LOVE TO THE CHURCH

1. The eternal love of Christ

The statement in the text points back — "Christ loved the Church". It points to what accounts for all provision and all action of grace bearing upon the Church. It speaks of Jehovah the Son, as set apart for the Church, as Messiah, to be its covenant Head, to be its Kinsman, to be its Redeemer, to be its Husband and to be its Saviour. It is the love of Him who was thus set apart to which our attention is called. That Christ loved the Church is a fact on which faith has always been wont to feast, and in which the ransomed of the Lord, with their perfect vision in heaven, shall find fathomless depths of wonder and enjoyment. It is a fact which never began to be [i.e. it was without beginning] — and yet it may be associated with every moment of time from the beginning to the end. Yea, it exists as a fact throughout all eternity, whether to our thinking eternity be past or future. But time is not, as we usually think of it, a line extending between, and separating, two eternities. It is rather an arc projected from (in order to return into) the one eternity which is the duration of Jehovah's being and is the sphere of His presence. That arc is the duration of the product of God's power in creation and the appointed season of His providence bearing on the earth and its inhabitants. How solemn is our position thus always near eternity and always about to enter eternity! But how sweetly overwhelming it is to think that out of all eternity, filled with the presence of Jehovah the Son, the glory of the wondrous love of Christ shines out upon the Church on earth.

The text tells us more than that there was love in Christ from everlasting — it tells us that He actually loved. We have assurance of this from His own mouth. He tells us that He was set up from everlasting, and that then He was rejoicing in the habitable parts of the earth, and that His delights were with the sons of men (Proverbs 8:23, 31). Christ was then loving His Church. His love was active even then in consenting to be set up as the covenant Head of His people, and in rejoicing in them as they were present to His eternal mind. How overwhelming in its infinite sweetness and wondrousness is this truth! And it intensifies one's wonder to think that this His joy in His loved ones on earth was always coincident with His joy, as Son, in the presence of His Father. How could the Church be admitted into the thoughts of Christ, as He was in that sphere of ineffable glory and blessedness? How could delight with these find a place in the heart that was filled with the joy of the Father's fellowship? But He is careful to place both joys together in His Word, in order to assure us that they were together in His heart. And both are perfectly consistent. Yea, because of the one there must be the other. The gladness arising from the enjoyment of the Father's love secures His loving acceptance of the people whom the Father gave Him. And to His infinite love, as Son, there was joy in the fulfilment of the Father's pleasure, and the manifestation of the Father's glorious name in the salvation (always present to His mind) of the people whose Surety He undertook to be. Is it not blasphemous to imagine that the love of Christ could have borne to be without these grounds of gladness in connection with all its objects?

But what conception can we form of this loving from everlasting? And how little we can bear to realise of it even by faith! When His Godhead and Sonship together with eternity come — associated with His love — into our hearts, how sweetly overwhelming is one moment of this power from on high!

Next (in historical sequence) to this eternal loving is His loving throughout all the past ages of time from the beginning. To dwell on this now would be to anticipate what awaits to be considered at a subsequent stage of our consideration of the text; for, in that event, we would have to speak of the outflow of His grace in salvation to the Church. But, following the order of the arrangements of the great scheme of redemption in their bearing on the purposed issues of that scheme, we must think next of His fulfilment of His promise to the Father in coming to be incarnate. "Lo, I come: in the volume of the book it is written of

Me, I delight to do Thy will, O My God: yea, Thy law is within My heart" (Psalm 40:7-8) is His own announcement of His promised advent. And this just puts Him into the position in which He can give the great expression of His love, to which the next statement of the text refers.

2. The object of Christ's love — His Church

The Church is the object of Christ's love. Those — and only those — who were effectually called are declared to be loved, and therefore to be known by themselves and others as the elect of God; though all who are to be called, in course of time, are known to God as such. It is in their effectual calling their condition was first affected by the love of Christ. Their calling was a necessary result of their being loved, and was secured also by the promise of the Father to His anointed. "Thou shalt call a nation that Thou knowest not, and nations that knew not Thee shall run unto Thee" (Isaiah 55:5). To Christ a seed was destined, and it was promised that He shall see His seed — that He shall see of the travail of His soul, and shall be satisfied — and that by His knowledge (the knowledge of Himself given by Him in effectual calling) shall My righteous servant justify many. And all this is sure, because the pleasure of the Lord shall prosper in His hand (Isaiah 53:10).

3. Reasons why people oppose the doctrine of election

Why is there such an aversion to thinking of the love of Christ as love to the Church, and not as love to all?

(a) To some minds this seems to be a minishing, as well as a limiting, of the love of Christ. They think they magnify the love by spreading its regards. One, having a little lake in his grounds, might, by shallowing it, desire to make it cover a larger area and thus make it seem to be of greater volume; but the quantity of water, notwithstanding of the increased expanse, would remain unchanged. He conceived no such project when looking on the ocean. Thinking of its measureless volume and of its fathomless depths, he was quite content with its expanse. It is thus as to men's conceptions of the love of Christ. When they fail to know it in connection with His personal glory, and have but slight views of the sinfulness of its objects, it is to them like the little lake to which they fain would give a shallow breadth. But those who know God and sin and Christ have before them, in the love of Christ, an ocean whose volume and depth are infinite; and they are content that the purpose of the Lord of all should define its expanse. A little thing for all, not a great thing for some, is what these others crave. Universality is the one great thing which they can associate with

45

it; and therefore, to make the love respectable, they choose to think of it as love to all.

(b) Others would fain that the love of Christ were universal in its saving purpose, that they might not have to think of its sovereignty. To think of it as an electing love is to be constrained to think that all depends on the will of God. They would fain that their own will had the sway in disposing of issues, and not that of God. They dislike to hear from the throne of the eternal Sovereign the words, "I will have mercy on whom I will have mercy" and to learn from His Word the lesson, that salvation is "not of him that willeth, nor of him that runneth, but of God that sheweth mercy" (Romans 9:15-16). They rather think of God as so compassionate that He cannot but be disposed to save the lost — and of the lost as having, in their misery, a claim on His pity — forgetting, or choosing to overlook, His words, "I will have compassion on whom I will have compassion" (Romans 9:15). He claims a sovereign power over the yearnings of His pity and assures the objects of His love that, being death-deserving sinners, they must owe all to His mercy.

(c) Others, still, like to think of Christ's love as universal (and not as love to those who are, and were, and shall be in the Church) that they may take comfort from it, while remaining in their natural state, thus having hope without being effectually called to Christ by being born again of God. With what intense readiness will a sinner who has become uneasy under a sense of danger receive the statement that "God is love", as implying that He certainly loves him even as he is, and now. He very eagerly substitutes this aspect of God's character for that which the law presented. And he will open all his old heart, under the sway of its selfishness, to receive an assurance of love instead of a fearful looking for of judgment, if his mind is so benighted and his conscience so unfaithful as to allow him to do so. And what a sudden change such faith as this will effect on his soul, though it be faith in a lie! What gladness now is his, when a fancied love hides from him the stern aspect of wrath! And under the impression thus produced there may appear in his exercises a counterfeit of all the graces of the Spirit, which may not be exposed till the midnight cry is heard and the door is shut.

(d) There are some who cannot receive the doctrine of universal love, and who at the same time feel as if, because it is electing love, there can be no hope for them. They cannot accept the doctrine of universal love because they feel that it would be dishonouring to God to ascribe to Him a love bearing upon sinners the certain issue of which would not be salvation; because the covenant arrangements springing from His love would thus be utterly invalidated; and

46

because such a passage as the text — and there are not a few such in Scripture — expressly confines His love and its outflow in saving grace to His chosen. But why should this discourage any soul that would fain be embraced by the love of Christ? Does not the sovereignty of the love make it all the more desirable to have an interest in it, for you may associate with this the certainty of everlasting salvation? And as it is the secret will of God which defines the purpose and reference of His love, this cannot be the rule of your faith. You have to be guided by what the Word of God tells you of this love as saving love to sinners. You have the character of Christ as unfolded in the great work of redemption, to act faith upon, and you are called to deal with the love, commended in the death of the cross. To this infinite saving love the authority of God shuts you up in the Gospel call — not as one loved, but as a wrath-deserving sinner who, if he comes to Christ, shall be embraced by that love and shall infallibly be saved with an everlasting salvation.

II. CHRIST GAVE HIMSELF FOR THE CHURCH

This is the great expression of Christ's love in behalf of the Church — He gave Himself for it. This refers to Christ's sacrificial work. True, we may think of His giving Himself in accordance with His Father's will to be in a position, as His people's Surety, in which He would give Himself for them as an atoning sacrifice. True, also, we may think of His actually giving Himself, as well as His being actually given by the Father, when in the fulness of the time He was on the earth, manifest in the flesh; but this was with a view to His giving Himself as an atoning sacrifice. If He was made flesh (John 1:14) it was with a view to His being made sin (2 Corinthians 5:21) and made a curse for His Church (Galatians 3:13).

In directing your attention to the words "gave Himself for it", we must consider the gift and the giving referred to in the action here ascribed to Christ, Him to whom the gift was presented, and the necessary immediate result of its being offered.

1. The gift

This is said to be Himself. It is not infrequently said that Christ's human nature was the sacrifice He offered, that His divine nature was the altar by which it was sanctified and that He, in both natures, was the High Priest by whom it was presented to God. But it were better to think (according to the text) of Himself in human nature as the sacrifice.

When we think of Him in human nature, we must think of Him as the Son, sent forth to redeem them that were under the law. He could not give Himself in human nature unto God as an atoning sacrifice till all was done and suffered by Him that availed to that effect. We must, on the one hand, be careful not to dissociate the sacrifice from Himself, and on the other hand not to separate it (in our thinking) from aught of all He went through in human nature during all His course of obedience and suffering, till both were closed and crowned in the death of the cross. And it is only when we connect both His person, with all its infinite dignity and blessedness, and His work, with all it implies of honour to the law and of satisfaction to justice, that we can rightly contemplate what was given by Him when He gave Himself for the Church. And we miss the link of connection between Himself and the sacrifice unless we find it in the words "for it". It was only because He was the Kinsman Surety of the Church that He could be made sin, and only because made sin that He could be made a curse. It was only because regarding Him as the representative of certain guilty persons that God could lay on Him their iniquities, and from Him, only as the Substitute of His people, could obedience be required. His obligation to obey was the result of the transfer to Him of the personal responsibility of those for whom He was Substitute. And His liability to suffer was the result of the transfer to Him of their personal guilt, as they were under the law as a covenant of works, and were accounted and condemned as its transgressors. Therefore, in the gift which He presented to God was all His obedience and suffering, with all the merit therein involved, because of the infinite dignity and blessedness belonging to Him as Jehovah the Son — and all this coming from Himself, in human nature, as the Substitute of the Church which God sent Him to redeem. O, what a gift this was! Conscience, are you satisfied with it? If not, your judgment is not according to the mind of God, for He has declared Himself to be well pleased.

2. The giving — Christ gave Himself

This calls our attention to the priestly action of Christ in giving Himself as an atoning sacrifice for the Church. He could only give Himself as an atoning sacrifice when under the power of death. "If so, how could He give Himself?" you may ask. Remember, friend, that it was as a sacrifice He died. He never died as a Priest, for He is a Priest according to the power of an endless life (Hebrews 7:16). He, in His eternal Godhead, lived to present Himself to God in human nature, as a slain sacrifice. His soul, separated from His body, and His body, separated from His soul, remained in union with His divine nature in His person as the Son. He offered Himself, therefore, when He presented before the throne of God the dead body that was laid in the grave of Joseph and the disembodied soul that went up to paradise in demonstration of His death. The Son of God did so, as the High Priest made with an oath after the order of Melchisedec (Hebrews 7:21). And O, think of such action as this — as the action of Jehovah the Son, called by the Father to give Himself for the Church! In this action appears divine zeal for the honour of the divine name, and divine love for the Church. He was bent on glorifying His Father and on His redeeming His Church; and He fully expressed even His zeal and love in the gift of Himself. O, my nature! what a halo of divine glory shines forth from thee, when I see thee slain in the person of the Son, who is the Lamb of God! Priestly action bearing on thee, as that of Him in whom thou didst subsist, shrouds thee in an ineffable brightness of glory — and glory to God in the highest shines up to heaven through thy rending!

3. Christ offered Himself to the Father

He received His commission as Christ from the Father, as the sovereign representative of the Godhead. And in the relation constituted by this commission, He was, on the earth, a Servant to Him who sent Him. But the work given Him to do was the redemption of the Church, and in that work He was a Surety in relation to God as Judge, as surely as He was a Servant in relation to God as Sovereign. His action as High Priest bore on the claims of God as Judge and in the perfect satisfaction of the Judge's claims there was a perfect fulfilment of the Sovereign's pleasure. O, think of what it was to God to receive what Christ gave for His Church! All the glory of the atoning person was in the view of God; all the merit of His obedience and suffering in human nature, in the light of that glory, was before His mind. Because, to fill His zeal for His own glory, through this sacrifice came an infinite vindication and display of His name. And all His claims were fully met. How infinitely well pleased was the Judge of all the earth! And, as Judge, His infinite delight in the sacrifice of Christ completed the opportunity for the fulfilment of all the behests of His love. Oh, what a sweet smelling savour there came to God from the sacrifice presented for the Church!

4. The result of Christ's giving Himself for the Church

The immediate result of Christ's giving Himself for the Church was threefold.

(a) God accepted the sacrifice

There must have been at once the acceptance by God of the sacrifice as offered in behalf of the Church. This acceptance was declared in Christ being raised from the dead by the glory of the Father.

(b) The exaltation of Christ

This was followed by His being exalted to the right hand of the Majesty in the heavens. Thus, not only was there a demonstration of the divine acceptance of Christ's sacrifice, but a full reward given to Him in human nature for the work which, in that nature, He finished on the cross.

(c) Christ was crowned "The Prince of Peace"

And because His sacrifice was given and accepted for the Church, He, in His relation to that Church, was crowned "The Prince of Peace". He has all power in heaven and on earth, all the gracious provision of the covenant which He sealed by His blood, and the seven Spirits of God, that He may reach with saving power, and enrich with saving blessings, His people all over the earth, and in every time of need, throughout all their wilderness life.

III. THE OUTFLOWING OF CHRIST'S LOVE

The outflow of Christ's love was to those for whom He gave Himself, that He might sanctify and cleanse it with the washing of water by the Word. Rendered exactly according to the grammatical construction of the original, this statement would read thus: "That He might sanctify it, having washed it with the washing of water, by the Word." According to this rendering, the washing comes before the sanctifying — and with either or with both, the Word may be connected, as the one appointed instrument used in this work of grace.

1. Christ cleanses His people from their sins

Christ washes His blood-bought people with the washing of water. This water is not the water used in baptism — it is rather that of which that water is an emblem. It is that of which the water of separation under the law was a type — it is the clean water, which the Lord promises to sprinkle, in order to cleanse from all filthiness and idols; it is that which is associated with the Spirit by Christ, in describing the new birth to Nicodemus; it is the living water of which Christ spake to the woman of Samaria; it is that by which the washing of regeneration is effected; it is what is done by the Spirit of God in beginning to apply the redemption purchased by Christ to those who were given to Him by the Father. He *does* then wash them with the washing of water. He comes as the living water, through the channel of Christ's merits, to apply what His sacrifice secured to those for whom it was offered. He comes as the Spirit of bondage to the subjects of His work, not to cause bondage but to make them feel the bondage of their state as sinners under the law. He comes as the Spirit that quickeneth, to implant the life of God — a germ of all holiness — within them in their regeneration. And He comes as the Spirit of faith, to lead them out of themselves to Christ, as revealed and offered in the Gospel, that they, being in Him, might be made the righteousness of God. Thus, they have in them a new man of God's creating, and are entitled to receive grace to preserve and to cherish and to cause it to grow till, fully sanctified, they attain to be holy, as God is holy. Thus, the washing leads, and secures a title, to the sanctifying.

2. Christ sanctifies His people

Christ's love to the Church is expressed in its sanctification. This is a progressive work, extending from regeneration till death. It is the carrying on of the work begun in regeneration, by the grace to which all who are justified and adopted are entitled, according to the covenant and promise of God. It is a work which pervades the whole man, in order to an entire renewal according to the image of God. The agent in this work is the Holy Ghost. He acts, as the Spirit of Christ, on the ground of His sacrifice, and as coming from the Father in response to His intercession, while at the same time freely expressing His own divine love in His work. Christ is sanctification (1 Corinthians 1:30) to the Church, as surely as the Spirit is its Sanctifier; for in His work the Spirit takes and applies what is Christ's. And while the Holy Ghost carries on His secret renewing work in the soul of the sanctified, He employs the Word in this work of transformation. He uses it as the mirror in which the Church can see its need of being sanctified. This use of the Word — in the demands of the holy law, in the example of Christ, and in the recorded attainments of the saints — cannot be dispensed with. But He uses it also as the warrant for repairing to Christ for the cleansing which He has the right and the power and the will to bestow through His blood and by the baptism of the Holy Ghost. And He uses it as the glass in which, beholding the glory of the Lord, the Church is changed into the same image, from glory to glory (2 Corinthians 3:18), till it is ready for Christ's presenting it to Himself.

IV. THE RIPE FRUIT OF CHRIST'S LOVE

This is seen in the final condition of the Church — "That He might present it to Himself a glorious Church, not having spot, or wrinkle, or any such thing; but that it should be holy and without blemish." Oh, what a finale this is! Poor leper, it is no wonder that you are often afraid that you shall never come to such an end as this. You are not able to conceive of this — it is so high, and you often feel as if to expect this would be to expose yourself to righteous contempt. But let us now think of what might be expected from such love as Christ's, and what He can accomplish — and whatever be awaiting the Church in its final condition, in the ripe fruit of Christ's love, you shall have as your own, if you are willing to be a debtor to the love that passes knowledge.

1. Christ shall present the Church to Himself

At the end Christ shall present the Church to Himself. It is like the Good Shepherd so to do. Before presenting it to the Father, He might be expected to present it to Himself, that it might appear before Him as the Father would have it to be and as He promised to make it. Oh, what enjoyment shall Christ have in it then! Not one member is awanting, and nothing is awanting to any one member, in soul or body, of the whole Church of God, redeemed, washed and sanctified on the earth. What infinite joy this will give to Christ's love to the Church, and what infinite enjoyment to the Son's love to His Father! He has His loved Church in a condition of perfect holiness, on the threshold of an eternity of blessedness and glory — and in bringing it to this He caused the Father's pleasure fully to prosper, and His name to be glorified. Oh, shall I be among them in whom, in all the intensity of a twofold infinite love, Christ shall at the end be glad?

(a) The presented Church will be glorious. Its glory will consist in its perfect conformity to Christ Himself. This is a glorifying to which it must attain before passing into heaven. Only a glorious Church can enter into a state of glory. It is the Spirit's work in sanctifying the soul on earth and in changing the vile body on the resurrection morning that can make the Church thus glorious. Glorious! Is it to come to this with you, poor, vile, loathsome leper? You cannot realise it as possible, and you are far, far from hoping that this end can be yours. But would you fain have it? And would you be a debtor to the love of Christ for this? If so, to this — to all this — you shall yet attain. What a wonder to yourself you shall be then, but all your wonder you will express in a song of praise for ever, to Him that loved you, and washed you from your sins in His own blood!

There are two passages of Scripture which make it plain that conformity to Christ is what makes the Church glorious. One is the grand passage — "Whom He did predestinate, them He also called, and whom He called, them He also justified, and whom He justified, them He also glorified" (Romans 8:30). The glorifying which is here declared to follow justifying must refer to the process and result of sanctifying. The other passage is that in which the gradual process of transformation into the image of the Lord is described as an advance from glory to glory (2 Corinthians 3:18).

(b) But this is not counted enough as a description of the final condition of the Church. It is said to be without spot. No stain of sin is left on it. O, will it come to this? No darkness left in the understanding, no rebelliousness in the will, no bondage and no unfaithfulness in the conscience, not the slightest tendency to depart from the living God in the heart, and nothing arising in the memory except what ministers to one's joy! Surely this is exceeding abundantly above all that we ask or think.

(c) But even this is not all — the Church shall be without wrinkle. There may be wrinkles on the heart, as well as on the brow, and the lack of renewing its age will soon occasion wrinkles on the heart of the Church while it is on the earth. Backsliding always causes wrinkles by provoking the removal of the Spirit's refreshing influences. Wasting sickness, as well as old age, may bring wrinkles on one's brow; so may the ailments which it brings on itself cause wrinkles on the heart of the Church. But all these shall be finally removed. "I will heal your back-sliding" (Jeremiah 3:22) was the Lord's promise, and He will do as He has said.

(d) But even this is not enough. "Nor any such thing" is added. If you can conceive of any thing besides spot or wrinkle, that would be well away — that would stand in the way of being perfectly well, and perfectly blessed — then that, whatever it be, Christ shall fully and for ever remove from His Church. Oh, is it not like Him so to do? What else could you expect from His infinite and holy love, moving omnipotence to fulfil its behests?

(e) But even all this is not yet enough. The Spirit tells us not only of the removal of all that would be a drawback, but tells besides of what shall be actually attained by the Church in the positive aspect of its final condition; for He adds these words to what was said before, "but that it should be holy". This is the consummation to which the Lord is pledged to bring the Church. All inconsistent with this is removed, but it is not a blank that is the result. There is all the positive purity of perfect holiness in the Church's attainment at last. Perfect love to God fills its whole being. It is perfectly like to God. Oh, what is higher than this? And to this Christ is pledged to bring the Church!

(f) But not even with this is the description of the Church's final condition closed, for it is declared that it shall be without blemish. There may have been blemishes that were not spots to be seen in some members of the Church on earth. I have known not a few who were heirs of glory, but who were idiots, knowing nothing but the spiritual lessons which they learned from God. These wayfaring men, though fools, did not err (Isaiah 35:8), but remained as simpletons among the wise of this world to the end, though taking rank before God among those who are made wise unto salvation. But no such blemish shall attach to them at the end. Lack of intellect disqualified them from prominent service in the Church on earth, but it will not remain as a drawback in heaven. No feebleness of intellect shall unfit them for the work above, nor will it remain to mar their blessedness. I have known, too, some godly ones with blemished bodies. Some I knew who were blind, some deaf, some lame, others paralytic, others still deformed, and some whose flesh was devoured by cancer till their bones were bare. But all such blemishes as these shall be removed. The risen body shall be perfect, as the soul is perfect — and perfect both shall be because they shall be conformed to the human nature of Christ. O, surely there is nothing left to complete the description of the final condition of the Church? There is nothing more for the Spirit of Christ to tell, nothing beyond for the love of Christ to desiderate, nothing further for the power of Christ to accomplish.

PRACTICAL APPLICATION

I must ask each one of you all, "Have you fellowship with the Church in the person, love, atonement, and salvation of Christ, and in the glorious prospect before it?" Surely this is an important question, with which only a fool will trifle. I would indicate various classes among you to whom I put this question, though in relation to an interest in the love of Christ I know among you only two: those who have it, and those who have it not.

1. There are some of you who live as if you were bent on proving to all who know you that the love of Christ has never reached you as saving grace. You care not to be embraced or saved by it. You never pause in your course of sin to think of it. You feel as if you could get on without it. Yea, you feel and act as if there was no such one as Christ, and no such love as His. And you are not afraid of being left thus far off to the end. Engrossed with cares as to things present around you in the world, you allow not yourselves to forecast the eternal future

before you. But you cannot always continue as you are. You will soon have to leave behind you all that you were putting into Christ's place in your thoughts and desires. And all you have from them, when you part with them, shall be the disappointment which will leave an aching void in your heart, the guilt they helped to accumulate, and the ripeness for destruction which they were the means of your attaining. Then shall come a felt calamity, out of which you must be persuaded that only Christ can deliver you. You will begin to call on Him when it is all too late. O, what will it be when He, the only one who can help, fulfils the threat of the awful words, "I also will laugh at your calamity; I will mock when your fear cometh; when your fear cometh as desolation, and your destruction cometh as a whirlwind; when distress and anguish cometh upon you. Then shall they call upon Me, but I will not answer; they shall seek Me early, but they shall not find Me" (Proverbs 1:26-28). It is surely sufficiently awful to be outside the love of Christ, but who can conceive of what the added awfulness is of being overwhelmed by His wrath! But know that if this shall be your end, it is only because you hated know-ledge, and did not choose the fear of the Lord (Proverbs 1:29); only because when Christ called, ye refused; when He stretched out His hand, none of you regarded (Proverbs 1:24).

2. There are some of you who have no interest in the love and salvation of Christ, and you know you have not — and yet this causes you little anxiety. How can you know what you do know and yet be easy? You know that you have never passed through such a change — or such a change passed over you — as is indispensable in order to your being within the true Church of God. You know, too, that if you are not effectually called out of the world that lies in the wicked one you can never derive any benefit from the love of Christ. I don't ask you whether you are in the Church, because you already know you are not; but I ask you how can you endure to be apart from Christ, and to be without any ground of hope that you shall be effectually called to Him ere you die? I ask you this latter question because you know not what is implied in being away from the embrace of the love of Christ. It is to this that I would fain that you applied your thinking and your care. Oh, what a loss is wilfully incurred by you in depriving yourself, by your rejection of Christ, of all the fruits of His love exhibited in the text! For it is only your refusing to accept of Christ, and all this in Him, that can account for your loss. You owe only to yourself your loss, while all that would be gain to you you must owe to God. And forget not that you cannot go away from the embrace of Christ's love without having to face the terrors of His wrath. You could keep away from His love, but you cannot

(if you die as you are) keep away from His wrath. O, think of the madness of refusing to try what Christ can do for you, and choosing to risk an eternal trial of what He can do against you! And you doing this with so much light in your mind, and so much conviction in your conscience.

3. There are some among you who excuse their listlessness by referring to the sovereignty of divine love, and the utter helplessness of the fallen sinner. It is only to abuse them, by making them excuses for your sinful neglect, that you take to do with those doctrines at all. Have you come to Christ to ask Him if there was room in His love for you? Have you ever been pained by a sense of your helplessness because it came between you and reaching Him? If not, what right have you to refer to the election of God, or to your own ruin by the fall, as an excuse for remaining at ease in Zion? Only a madman could so act. A man with any measure of wisdom would consider that what seemed to exclude him from the bosom of Christ was so awful that to sleep in front of it would be utterly impossible.

4. There are some of you who, I fear, think that the comfort you have found in believing in the love of Christ to you, because of its being love to all, is evidence of your having obtained an interest in the love referred to in the text. Friends, one thing is certain that, if you have any right view of the love of Christ, it will draw you out towards the person of the lover. The benefit resulting from the love is not to be separated from the love that bestows it, nor can the love be separated from the person loving. To win Christ and be found in Him, is the desire prompted by right views of His love. And there cannot be enjoyment that is genuine in the love of Christ unless, in the light of the cross, you see how righteous and holy — as well as rich and free — it is. And if you are rightly affected by it, what you seek, as the fruit of Christ's love, will be what is described in the text. How is it with you as to this? O, friends, do not be satisfied with a false picture of the love that passeth knowledge (Ephesians 3:19) or with aught you may think you have as a benefit, which you have won by theft. Only in Christ, and through the blood of His cross, can you have any legitimate gain.

5. There are some among you who would fain be in the Church, to be folded in the embrace, and to be enriched by the fruits of Christ's love. Remember that ere Christ could have a Church to love, He had to call it effectually unto Himself out of the world that lieth in wickedness (1 John 5:19). His love, because it is love to the Church, must be love to sinners. To that love, as a sinner, you may therefore appeal. You may take Himself the lover, and thus get all the love of His heart and all the power of His hand, all the merit of His blood

and all the riches of His grace. And resting on Him, with all your case as a sinner, withhold not your heart from the joy of hoping that what He has promised to His Church shall yet be enjoyed by you. His love passeth knowledge (Ephesians 3:19), His blood cleanseth all who come to Him from all sin (1 John 1:7); for His power there is nothing too hard (Jeremiah 32:17), and His faithfulness never fails (Psalm 89:33). And in the measure in which you enjoy any rest on the bosom of Christ, remember what you were, and what you are, and do not forget to ascribe all glory to Him who remembered you in your low estate (Psalm 136:23).

The smitten Shepherd and His flock

Awake, O sword, against My Shepherd,
and against the man that is My fellow, saith the Lord of hosts:
smite the Shepherd, and the sheep shall be scattered: and I will turn Mine hand
upon the little ones.

ZECHARIAH 13:7

There are four remarkable verses quite near to one another in this and the preceding chapter. One of these is the first verse of this chapter in which appears the fountain opened for sin and uncleanness. The text informs us how that fountain was opened. In the tenth verse of the preceding chapter we are informed how sinners are led to the fountain, to be washed therein — even by the Spirit of grace and of supplications. And in the last verse of this chapter we are told how the Lord deals with those on whom the Spirit has been poured, till He at last brings them spotless and blessed out of all their tribulations.

In addressing you from this text, I will call your attention to:
I.   The Shepherd of the Lord of hosts and His flock;
II. The description given of His person;
III. The dealing of the Lord of hosts with His Shepherd;
IV. The results of the Shepherd having been smitten.

I. THE SHEPHERD OF THE LORD OF HOSTS AND HIS FLOCK

"My Shepherd," says the Lord of hosts. It is of Him whom He also says "My Fellow" that He thus speaks.

1. God appointed His own Son as Mediator

Jesus Christ is His Shepherd as Mediator; and as He stands between the Lord of hosts and His flock He is claimed from both sides. The Lord of hosts says "My Shepherd" — and David, one of His flock, says "my Shepherd". Think of the divine claim and the human, in the same words, meeting on the head of the same person!

Why did the Lord of hosts require a Shepherd? Because He had a flock to tend — a people whom He purposed to save. In order to fulfil His purpose bearing on them, He had to provide a Shepherd for them. None else was there to care for them. And even if there were, who could make a suitable provision for them? And even if there were one both able and willing to do so, who but the Lord was entitled to appoint a Shepherd? But before the foundation of the world was laid, the Lord set One apart to be His Shepherd for His flock.

2. God set His Son apart to be the Shepherd

"My Shepherd," says the Lord of hosts, for He set Him apart to that office. He it was who found a Shepherd for the flock. His was the name whose glory was to be manifested — His the justice whose demands were to be satisfied — His the law which was to be magnified — and His the flock which the Shepherd had to tend. And He engaged Him, in the name of the Godhead, as representing the sovereign authority of Jehovah. He gave Him His commission to act the Shepherd's part, and "Him hath God the Father sealed" (John 6:27). Well entitled, therefore, is the Lord of hosts to claim the Shepherd as His own.

3. God delights to have His Son as Shepherd

"My Shepherd," says the Lord of hosts, for He delights to have Him. Who can conceive what it is to the Lord of hosts, as the Father, to have Him so that He can call Him "My Beloved Son"? And who can conceive what it is to Him, as the Lord of all, whose pleasure is in Messiah's hands, to have Him so as to be entitled to call Him "My Shepherd"? And who can tell with what delight He, in His infinite love to His chosen people, contemplates Him in His relation to them? Before His view, in this wondrous Shepherd, is all that is required in order to His name being glorified in their everlasting salvation. That consummation is always present to the mind of God associated with Him whom He has appointed to be the great Shepherd of the sheep (Hebrews 13:20). In His sovereign authority He claims Him as His own; and in all the infinite intensity of His Fatherly love, in all His zeal for the glory of His name and in all His everlasting love to His people, He rejoices to have Him so that He may claim Him as His own.

4. God gave the flock to His Son

And this Shepherd has no flock except what the Father gave Him. "Thine they were," He says to the Father, "and Thou gavest them Me" (John 17:6). He gave them, as loved ones, whom it was His purpose to save. We cannot think that it was because they were sinners He loved them; nor can we approach to think that there was any good, in His view, associated with them, which drew forth His love. He loved their persons just because it so seemed good in His sight; and never will other reason be found for His electing love, either in time or in eternity. If a consideration of misery, causing the exercise of pity, accounts for salvation, then all must be saved; and if only by a consideration of goodness could love have been induced, then no one could be saved. It was as loved ones, who were sinners and whom it was Jehovah's purpose to save, that they were given by the Father (as the representative of the authority and resources of the Godhead) as a flock, to His Shepherd.

This flock was one company, as given by the Father to the Son — and shall be one company when finally presented by the Son to the Father. But, meantime, it is broken up into sections. There are two sections in heaven, two on earth, and one neither in heaven, earth or hell. There are a few — there are two individuals at any rate — if more, and if so, how many I cannot say — who are there in glorified bodies; and besides these, there are in heaven the spirits of the just made perfect. On earth there are some who have been effectually called into a state of grace and there are others who are as yet in a state of nature — other sheep, not yet of this fold (John 10:16). And there are many — we cannot but think, the largest section of the flock — neither born nor born again, who are neither in heaven nor on earth; and of all the flock, none ever was in hell — and none ever shall be in hell.

But they were all given to Christ with a view to their salvation, and therefore they were all given to Him as sinners. And He knew them all as such. He knew all that He was required to do and to endure, with a view to their redemption. He knew what had to be done in order to their being gathered into the fold, that He might have them and know them as His sheep, they having and knowing Him as their Shepherd. He knew all, too, that was implied in His caring for them, guiding them, feeding and healing them, and at last bringing them spotless to their place in glory. And He with infinite willingness undertook to be their Shepherd! Sing His praise, though it should be in very feeble bleating, all ye who are the sheep of His pasture!

Let us make a very extravagant supposition, for without doing so we can find no illustration that can help to indicate the greatness of Messiah's undertaking as the Shepherd of the Lord of hosts. Suppose someone, who wished to procure a shepherd, had advertised for one, and that in reply to his advertisement, a person appeared before him, and accepted the wages which were offered and was engaged. The shepherd asks to be shown the flock and to be told what he is expected to do. It is all too late to ask this now, for the man would never have engaged him if he had asked this before. He is shown an enclosure within which is the flock, the entrance to which is guarded by a force that will admit no one within the fence who does not pay a ransom in blood. Looking through the gate the new shepherd can see nothing but heaps of bones covering the enclosed ground, and wild beasts prowling among the heaps and feasting on the bones. "What am I to do?" he asks his master. "You must pay the ransom. You must destroy these wild beasts. You must bring these bones to life. You must bring them as living sheep out of the enclosure in which they are. You must take care of them thereafter, and see that they are fed and healed. And you must bring them to me, all whole and all without blemish — and then your wages shall be paid." This hireling thought only of the wages when he was engaged as shepherd; he forgot about the work, and seeing that the first thing must be to lay down his life ere he could have a flock to tend, he soon fled, turning his back right speedily, both on the master and the flock. I said that I was going to make an extravagant supposition, and I have surely done in this instance according to my promise. But all the extravagance is yet too little to indicate the greatness of the Good Shepherd's work.

All in the flock, given to His Shepherd by the Lord of hosts, were under arrest, as criminals, and condemned to die; and He had to buy them by His blood. They were spiritually dead in trespasses and sins, and He had to quicken them by His Spirit. They were under the fell power of Satan with his hosts of spirits of darkness, and his vast army in the world, all bent on serving him as the murderer of souls; and He had to deliver them by His power. And they had, after being quickened and gathered, to be preserved from all destroyers, and to be fed and healed and guided, till at last they all were brought with gladness into glory. This was Christ's undertaking; and as this was all needed by the flock, it was not too much, either for His love or for His power.

II. THE DESCRIPTION GIVEN OF HIS PERSON

The Lord of hosts calls Him "the man that is My fellow". These are wondrous words from the mouth of the Lord of hosts. One who is a man He calls His fellow. Surely the name of Him, whom He thus addresses, is "the Wonderful" (Isaiah 9:6).

1. The human nature of Christ

"The man" He is, for Christ has true human nature subsisting in His person. He had a real human body and a real human soul; He was conceived and He was born; and He had all the sinless infirmities of human nature attached to the flesh and blood of which He partook.

This made Him the kinsman of all whose Shepherd he engaged to be, and gave Him an opportunity of acting as their Surety. He could, as the man, take their place under the law, as a covenant, to do and to die for them. And it gave Him joy to know Himself both as the kinsman and the Surety of the people whom the Father gave Him. He appeared often in human nature, under the Old Testament dispensation, loving to be near His people in order to speak to them with human lips. He loved the brotherhood this gave Him in relation to His beloved ones; or, as someone once said, "He loved to try on the dress beforehand in which He was to appear in the fulness of time as God manifest in the flesh". And when the fulness of the time came, hear His glad shout, "Lo, I come to do thy will, O God" (Hebrews 10:9); "a body hast Thou prepared Me" (Hebrews 10:5). How often He called Himself "the Son of man" when He was on the earth; and how careful He was to appear in human nature, in the act of ascension to heaven, to assure His disciples that He was to have it there in the midst of the throne for ever.

And the Father loved to look on Him as the man Christ Jesus. As such, all was seen in Him which was required for the accomplishment of His redemptive purpose bearing on the objects of His love. He delighted in seeing His Beloved Son the kinsman of His beloved people; as well as in contemplating what should arise to Himself of glory, and flow out to them of grace, because of the work to be done by One who was a partaker (in its perfect purity) of the very nature through which came, in the first Adam, dishonour to His name and ruin to the race of mankind.

And with what unspeakable delight ought we to feast our eye (and through our eye our heart) on the man of whom the text speaks. We have to look back on one — Adam — who was our covenant head, and who in transacting with God in our behalf, ruined both himself and us. How can we, in our meanness, out of the depths in which the fall has plunged us, lift up our eye directly to the holy majesty of Jehovah? But O, what is it to have One to look to, who is Mediator between God and men, and is the man Christ Jesus! How delightful is the veil of His flesh tempering the light of the awful glory of Jehovah! And what bliss to know that the fulness of the Godhead, in the person of Him who is the man, becomes an infinite fountain! And out of this fountain, into His work as the kinsman Surety, comes infinite merit to make it all that I, as a sinner, require in order to have peace with God and to have access to His presence! The more I realise the glory of Jehovah in my Elder Brother, the more I am encouraged to approach Him — for I know that because of His infinite riches of glory, He has infinite riches of merit to meet my guilt and infinite riches of grace to meet my poverty.

And how sweet to our hearts it should be to follow the man through all the experience of trial which made Him a man of sorrows, and gave Him the power of sympathy which kinship and suffering alone could have given Him! He must have been in all points tempted like as we are, ere He could be touched with a feeling of our infirmities (Hebrews 4:15). But O! think of Him as now in the midst of the throne, with His perfect memory of all His suffering, seeing the accordance in all points between what He endured and what is experienced of trial by His people, and associating with every exercise of His power in helping them, what makes it both the fruit of infinite divine love and an expression of perfect human sympathy.

2. The divine nature of Christ

"My fellow," says the Lord of hosts regarding Him who is His Shepherd and the man. This is one of the most striking ways in which in all Scripture the wonderfulness of Christ's person, as Emmanuel, is presented to us.

The word rendered "fellow" here occurs besides only in the book of Leviticus. There it occurs repeatedly and is always rendered "neighbour"; and so thoroughly relative a term is it, that it is never found without a suffix. It is applied in Leviticus to one who was of the same blood, the same people, the same tribe, the same locality with another. There must have been kinship and nearness to constitute one the "fellow" or "neighbour" of another. These ideas we must transfer to the relation which this word indicates between the Lord of hosts and His Shepherd.

He cannot be acknowledged as His fellow by the Lord of hosts without His being a partaker of the divine nature. He is so, necessarily and eternally, as a person who is God, for there can be no divine person not equal to the other divine persons. The divine nature is one and undivided and indivisible, and subsists in its infinite fulness in each. O, what is it to have Jehovah as my Shepherd! — the fellow, in respect of equality, of Him who, as the Lord of hosts, is my Judge! Jehovah on my side, in my kinsman, who is engaged in atoning work! O, my soul, there is hope for you after all; for a divine person is the Surety of the unjust! And He is one with the Lord of hosts as surely as He is His equal. He is in the Father and the Father in Him; and as the Lord of hosts from heaven calls Him "My fellow", so He on the earth said, "I and My Father are one" (John 10:30). And He is in a most intimate relationship of love to Him who claims Him as His Shepherd; for He is His eternal only begotten Son. Who can conceive of what the intimacy and love of this relation is? And what heart can contain the delight occasioned by knowing that one who is a kinsman stands in such a relation to the Lord of hosts?

And this fellowship of the Shepherd with the Lord of hosts refers to their intimate association in the great scheme of redemption. One in love, both must be equally interested in the fulfilment of the purpose of salvation bearing on the elect. If the Shepherd has come, it was the Father who sent Him. If He carried on and finished the work of redemption, the Father upheld Him during its process. His gathering of the flock is the Father's drawing. All He does in defending, guiding and healing them is connected with the Father's blessing them with all spiritual blessings. If He baptises with the Holy Ghost, it is because He has received the promise of the Spirit from the Father. And if He is "all in all" to His flock, it is because in Him it pleased the Father that all fulness should dwell. O, what ecstatic delight it gives to one's heart, to connect by faith this fellowship of the Mediator with the Father, and that which is His as Jehovah the Son! In His eternal divinity as the living God, in the exercise of His intercessory power as Priest, and in the potency of His reign as the Prince of Peace, we must not think of Him as the listless channel of the Father's grace, but as the earnest, ever loving, ever active fellow of the Father, accomplishing the pleasure of the Lord of hosts in the salvation of all whom He bought by His blood.

III. THE DEALING OF THE LORD OF HOSTS WITH HIS SHEPHERD

"Awake, O sword, against My Shepherd: smite the Shepherd."

1. The sword of divine justice

By the sword is indicated the weapon, or instrument, by which is executed the sentence passed by divine justice. The sword may be said to be the sword of divine justice, if we mean that it is that by which the judgment, awarded by divine justice, is executed; but we must not approach to say that divine justice is the sword. Even among men, the Judge never executes the sentence which he passes. In other days some great criminal was set apart for the hangman's work; and it was by executing the sentence passed on others that he escaped from enduring the sentence passed upon himself. It would be more according to truth to regard the arch-criminal, Satan, as the executioner than the Lord of hosts, for it is declared that he has the power of death, having hosts under him to accomplish his awful work in bringing his power to bear on those who are condemned to die. But whatever the blade and edge of the sword may be, around all its length and edge is the flame of divine wrath, which must burn into every wound which the stroke of the sword inflicts.

"Awake" and "smite" are the words addressed to the sword by the Lord of hosts. We are not to approach to thinking that these words are a justification of what is done by those who take part in the executioner's work. They certainly imply an approval of Jehovah's own judicial action — of this and of no more. No more, because although he who hath the power of death is allowed to act, he has no commission from heaven for the work in which he is engaged, and is earning death (in common with all the slaves who serve under him) while inflicting the sentence of death on others.

2. The sword awaking against the Shepherd

"Awake, O sword," says the Lord of hosts to the instrument of vengeance against sin; because the greatest work that ever was or ever could be done, in carrying out the awards of justice, has now to be done. The vengeance demanded on sin requires that the work be thoroughly done. Never was there work for the sword which executes the vengeance due, like that which lies before it. The countless sins of each one of a multitude whom no man can number have now to be atoned for, till the justice of the Lord of hosts is satisfied.

" 'Awake' though it is My Shepherd whom you have to smite — Him whom I have appointed to save a people whom I loved from everlasting." Think of Him bearing imputed sin — and think of the sins which He bears as the sins of God's chosen — and then think of how inflexible is the justice of the Lord of hosts.

" 'Awake' though He who is My Shepherd is the man that is My fellow. He, even He, must die the death, because He is the Shepherd of a flock of sinners." O, sinner, if this was said in reference to Him, what (apart from Him) can intercept from you the edge and flame of the devouring sword?

And what powers are brought into action in consequence of this summons? The power of hell and the power of the world — of which Satan is the prince — are to do their utmost in the work of judgment. But, in all the action of hell and of the world, He on whom the sentence of death is to be executed must know (as an expression of the wrath of God) all that these are permitted to do against Him in the course of providence. The sword must always be a flaming one as well as a piercing one in His experience.

3. The sword smiting the Shepherd

"Smite the Shepherd." Early began the smiting! The sentence was being executed all along His whole life in the flesh on earth; for all throughout He bore the imputed sins of His people and was suffering in consequence. He lived a man of sorrows because He was a sin-bearer and because in consequence the curse of the law was taking effect upon Him.

It was this which gave Him a stable as a birthplace and a manger as His cradle. It was this that caused his flight to Egypt, to escape from the cruelty of murderous Herod. It was this that caused the obscurity and poverty of His home in Nazareth. It was this that caused His experience of persecution because of the first sermon which He preached and which, but for a miracle, would have ended in His death. It was this that accounted for His having no place whereon to lay His head, while the foxes had holes and the birds of the air had nests. It was this which exposed Him to all the storm of persecution which He encountered during all His public ministry. It was this which caused His agony in Gethsemane. It was this that accounted for His being betrayed by one disciple, denied by another and forsaken by all. It was this that caused the humiliation of His being before court after court, as if He were the most criminal of malefactors. It was this which made Him the reproach of the people and the butt of cruel Roman soldiers. It was this that caused Him to be led forth from Jerusalem under the burden and reproach of the cross.

But the summons still is "Smite!". O, has not all that is past been enough? All this as the experience of the man who is the fellow of the Lord of hosts might surely suffice for Him. For Him, do you say? Why, there was nought of all such experience as this due to Him! To Him belong blessing and honour and glory and power (Revelation 5:13); but to the people, whose Surety He was, dishonour and distress and death were due. He is experiencing according to their deserts. Therefore the summons still is "Smite!". Smitten to death He must be! The justice of the Lord of hosts demands this. The mad rage of hell, and the furious enmity of graceless men of no religion, and of graceless men of much religion, cry out for this. Both combine in the cry, "Crucify Him, crucify Him!". And your redemption, believer, required His being smitten, till His soul and body were parted in dying. Hell's greatest feat, which proved to be the utter defeat of its power — the most awful murder — the killing of the Prince of Life by the hands of wicked men — the full endurance of the law's penalty for satisfaction to divine justice — the slaying of the Lamb of God in order to there being a sacrifice to God for a sweet smelling savour — the payment in His own blood of the ransom price, in order that the Shepherd may buy His flock — all this must take place. And the smiting dead of the man who is the fellow of the Lord of hosts is the event — the only one — in which all this could be involved. O yes! the Word of God has taken effect, and the result is that His Beloved Son is on the accursed tree, in a lifeless body, which passed through torturing agony ere it parted with the soul, whose agony was greater still. Yes, Beloved, Thou wert smitten because Thou wouldst that Thy flock should live; and Thine was no vain display of love, for peace through Thy chastisement and healing through Thy stripes shall be theirs (Isaiah 53:5).

IV. THE RESULTS OF THE SHEPHERD HAVING BEEN SMITTEN

"The sheep shall be scattered: and I will turn Mine hand upon the little ones."

1. The sheep shall be scattered

This is distinctly applied by Christ to the desertion of Him by His disciples at the time of His crucifixion. We cannot therefore but feel persuaded that here, in the prophecy, there was a reference to what is there in the history.

Yes, the sheep are scattered. In this day of storm and tempest the Shepherd alone could stand — and the Shepherd stood alone. Of the people there was none with Him at any stage of His work as Surety (Isaiah 63:3), and He must be manifestly alone when He is finishing it on the cross. I am not to excuse the desertion of Him by His disciples — but I rejoice in the providence of God, according to which the Beloved is solitary when He is redeeming the flock given to Him by His Father by pouring out His soul unto death.

Let none of us dare, in a self-complacent spirit, to condemn those deserters. How often, without any such fiery trial as that through which they had to pass, have we ourselves forsaken Him? But we are always more prone to strike on the sores of others than to smite upon our own breasts. There are not a few who are like the horse-fly that finds its choicest sustenance in sores. It seems to be with the appetite of this kind of insect that these fly over the record of the Bible, to alight on the faults of the saints and to deepen them. As they follow their hell-born instinct, these blood-suckers may find what shall make them strong to despise true godliness and increase their contentment without it; but in gaining this, they have won only what it is a judgment to acquire. They need not boast of their might or their wisdom, who have power and skill only to attain what must yet add to their misery.

I am not concerned as to the work in which the Shepherd is engaged, because He is left alone. He is able all alone to finish it. And the desertion of Him by the sheep tells us that beside Him, or besides Him, there is none to look to for redemption. All have been driven away by the storm except Himself; but when the tempest is at its wildest, the shout is heard from the solitary sufferer on the cross, "It is finished".

Are the sheep scattered? Then let all in the flock of the Good Shepherd, in every age and place, learn their dependence on the Shepherd's gracious care to preserve them, as well as their dependence on His death to redeem them. Did these forsake Him? Then surely you may; and if the Lord does not preserve you, the smallest trial will suffice to scare you away from His fellowship and service.

This scattering of the disciples, though evidently alluded to, may point our attention, further on, even to the scattering of the whole people of the land, who regarded themselves as the sheep of the Shepherd whom the Lord promised to Israel. This scattering of the disciples may be regarded as a prelude of the other (and more extensive) scattering, when threatened judgments would overtake the nation by whom Messiah was denied and crucified. Or may it not point to the dispersion (because of national judgments) of the faithful witnesses, the true sheep of the Good Shepherd, in order to spread among all nations the savour of His blessed name? Works of judgment occasioned the scattering of these sheep but purposes of grace were fulfilled by their dispersion. In this scattering of the sheep, the Lord found an opportunity of turning His hand upon the little ones.

2. The Lord will deal graciously with His own flock

"I will turn mine hand upon the little ones."

The words, "I will turn my hand" are sometimes used to describe divine action in a work of judgment, and at other times to describe a change of dealing in beginning a work of grace. In this latter sense it is to be understood in the promise, "I will turn My hand upon thee, and purely purge away thy dross, and take away all thy tin" (Isaiah 1:25). This must be the meaning of this phrase in the text. It indicates a mode of dealing different from that of which the Shepherd had experience. And the description given of those on whom the Lord of hosts was to turn His hand makes this altogether certain. Those called "little ones" are tenderly referred to and shall be tenderly treated.

These little ones were undoubtedly (but not exclusively) the disciples who forsook the Shepherd and fled. How graciously was this fulfilled to them when the Lord of hosts raised the Shepherd from the dead! — when He secured to them, during forty days, occasional opportunities of converse with Him; and allowed them, at the close of that period, an opportunity of seeing Him go up to heaven. This was followed by an outpouring of the Spirit from on high, as the result of which the little ones rallied again, in the name of Jesus took their stand as witnesses before the powers of darkness — and in the face of a persecuting world. "Little ones" verily these were! How little when we think of the awakened sword, before which they were exposed in their guiltiness, and by which the Great Shepherd of the sheep was smitten! How little were these as compared with the man who was the fellow of the Lord of hosts! But they were the little ones who were cared for in love by God! O yes! He did care for them! They were the little ones of His love! How He delights in turning in His love towards them! while on the gift of His hand to them shines the brightness of the glory of all His name, as manifested in the smiting of the man who was His fellow.

But there were little ones, besides these, towards whom the love of the Lord of hosts went forth, and on whom He was to turn His hand in order to make them subjects of a work of grace. Among the little ones were all included in the flock given to the Shepherd, bought by His blood, but not yet effectually called by His Spirit. Towards these all He promises to turn His hand in the gracious ministration of the Spirit, according to the behests of His own love and in reward of Messiah's obedience unto death. On these He would turn His hand in order to bring them to the Shepherd. "No man," says Christ, "can come to Me, except the Father which hath sent Me, draw him" (John 6:44). And in joyful expectation of the Father's promise of drawing being fulfilled, He says, "All that the Father giveth Me shall come to Me" (John 6:37). And the result of their being drawn to Him is that they become one spirit with Him (1 Corinthians 6:17) and the righteousness of God in Him (2 Corinthians 5:21). This gives to the Lord of hosts an opportunity of placing them in such relation to Himself that He turns His hand on them in the exercise of His pardoning mercy. And their justification furnished the love of God with an opportunity of adopting them into His family, so that His dealing with them shall henceforth be that of a father with his children. O, what a turning of His hand is this! And the hand thus turned *on* them shall never be turned *from* them, for He has bound Himself by His promise not to turn away from them, to do them good (Jeremiah 32:40). According to that promise, He will follow up by a course of blessing (that shall extend over all their life) the good which He did to them when they were called and justified.

PRACTICAL APPLICATION

1. This text is well fitted to remind us of the words of Christ: "If they do these things in a green tree, what shall be done in the dry?" (Luke 23:31). How much more unlikely is the green tree to be affected by fire than the dry! And if the fire, which has greatly affected the former, comes in contact with the latter, how much more disastrous must the result be! But what does the text present to us? The holy One and the Just, who is the eternal Son of God, bears the imputed sins of a people whom Jehovah loved from everlasting; and the sword, by which vengeance is executed, is summoned to awake and smite Him. And awake it did, and it smote Him dead.

O sinner, what are you in your meanness, weakness, guiltiness, loathsomeness and proved hostility to God, that you should think of escaping from being devoured by the sword, if you have not found refuge under the blood of the smitten Shepherd? O poor worm, what must befall you if the sword is summoned to awake against you and to smite you! And smite you it shall, if you remain away from the Good Shepherd, and if the merit of His death is not placed to your account. You cannot dare to deny that you are guilty of transgressing the law of God, and that "cursed is every one that continueth not in all things which are written in the book of the law to do them" (Galatians 3:10). Surely, then, you cannot think as a rational being and give any credit to the truth of God's Word without coming to the conclusion that you yourself — your very self — are cursed; and that unless the curse, which now rests on you, be removed, you shall encounter all the awfulness of enduring the infliction of that curse for ever. And are you to remain easy in front of this? Are you still to run on towards it? Are you to rush on as if you were afraid the gate of hell would be closed before you could reach it? Such fear, friend, is a groundless one, if it exists, for you will — and soon, very soon — certainly reach, in an accursed death, the gate of an eternal hell, if you move on as you have been doing in the past. You care not for shelter from the storm which smote the Shepherd. You present yourself in your guilt and weakness right before it. O, how awful, in your experience, must the shock be when it strikes you outside the only shelter — the covert of the Great Shepherd's blood!

2. But to you as a sinner, as such a sinner as you are, there is a way of escape opened up before you in the text. There could be no possible escape for you if the justice of God were not fully satisfied. But the text shows you that it was satisfied by the death of the man who is the fellow of the Lord of hosts. And remember that He died for the ungodly. And as you look to Him acting the part of their Surety, you can see how every stroke by which He was smitten, as He was rendering satisfaction, was opening up a way through which you are called to flee to the bosom of God's everlasting mercy. O, friend, be not satisfied without seeing this with the eye of faith, to the wonder and joy of your heart!

There is much said in these days of finding peace, without the understanding being enlightened by the doctrine of the cross, without the will embracing the divine person who died on the cross, without the conscience being purged by the blood of the cross or the heart being affected by the power of the cross, and without any persuasion of the need of being regenerated and anointed by the Holy Ghost, in order that all this may be attained. But, friend, do not consent to a slight probing or to a slight healing of your wound by those who say, "Peace, peace; when there is no peace" (Jeremiah 6:14). Remember that your one way of deliverance from guilt is that presented by the doctrine of the cross. Remember that you can never appreciate what is revealed there without the teaching of the Holy Ghost. Remember that you must remain a child of darkness if the divine glory of the crucified One shine not into your soul. For only as you look on the death of the cross, under that light, can you find sufficient atonement for the purging of your conscience — and never be content to have conscience quieted without its first being purged as only divine blood

71

can purge it. Only as you look on the death of the cross can you discover love such as you, with all your unworthiness, may expect a full salvation with a welcome from God. Remember, too, that without vital union to the person of Christ you can have no benefit from His redemption; but that, while to effect that union is the work of the Holy Spirit, it is your duty to cast yourself on Jesus, even as you are — for the call of God in the Gospel makes it so. And if you do so, there shall be nought awanting on His side required to make it certain that you shall be one spirit with Him.

3. Are you looking wistfully to a place among the little ones, of whom the Shepherd of the Lord of hosts takes care? Well, friend, if you would fain be one of them, the way to attain this is, as a sinner, to accept the Shepherd to be yours. Take Him, as He is offered to you in the Gospel, and all that pertains to the flock shall be yours. What can you lack, if you have Him? Do not imagine that you will ever discover that you are one of the flock given to Him by the Father till first, as a child of wrath, you come to Him who was sent to seek and to save that which was lost. Let your calling be made sure and then — and only then — can your election be made sure. Your election must have been first as an act of God; and in the view of God that made your calling certain. But you have to rise from the dust and dunghill on which you were cast by the fall, through an effectual call, to the knowledge of that election of which all salvation is the fruit. Be content to take the place which the law shows you to be yours as a transgressor, and then receive Him to be your own, who came into the world to save sinners.

4. O what a feast is in this text for the sheep of the flock of which Messiah is the Shepherd! Here He is in the marvellous glory of His person, as the man who is Jehovah's fellow! Here He is in the infinite merit of the death He died! Here He is in matchless love! Here He is in the efficiency of His finished work — the Lord of hosts being pledged to put forth His power in order to give Him a satisfying reward of all His travail in the salvation of the little ones! O, friend, is there not enough here? especially when around all this and through it shines forth, in its highest and fullest manifestation, the glory of the Lord of hosts.

O seek grace to be more eager in desiring, and more diligent in partaking of this wonderous feast! O how little you have known, and trusted, and loved, and praised, and obeyed, and suffered for the man who is the fellow of the Lord of hosts! — who for your sins was smitten, that His chastisement might be the chastisement of your peace, and that you, through His stripes, might have healing! O cleave to Him! for He is your only refuge, your only guide, your only healer, the "friend that sticketh closer than a brother" (Proverbs 18:24). Seek to know His voice and to follow Him. Be content to pass even through the fire in His company. And seek to be so purged, as to be made ready for being with Him, as He is in the midst of the throne on high, so showing Himself from out of the glory in which He dwells, that He shall be recognised by you as the Lamb slain or as the Shepherd smitten — while His glory and His love shall so affect you that to sing His praise as your Redeemer shall be your blissful exercise for ever. And O! seek to be more and more lost in admiration of the glory of the Lord of hosts — the glory of His wisdom, truth, righteousness and love — and to be more hearty in your acknowledgements of what you owe to Him of whom are all things that reach you through the Great Shepherd of the sheep.

It is Finished

It is finished.

JOHN 19:30

In Matthew 27:50 we read, "Jesus, when He had cried again with a loud voice, yielded up the ghost".

In Mark 15:37 we read, "And Jesus cried with a loud voice, and gave up the ghost".

In Luke 23:46 we read, "And when Jesus had cried with a loud voice, He said, Father, into Thy hands I commend My spirit: and having said thus, He gave up the ghost".

In John 19:30 we read, "When Jesus therefore had received the vinegar, He said, It is finished: and He bowed His head, and gave up the ghost".

Comparing all these accounts of His dying, we find them all telling us that "He gave up the ghost". The first three tell us that, ere He did so, "He cried with a loud voice". Luke and John tell us that, as a sign of His resignation in dying, "He bowed His head". Luke alone gives us His prayer in the act of dying. And John alone tells us what His articulate utterance was when He cried with a loud voice. It was evidently when He cried that He said "It is finished". These are the words which He uttered with a loud voice. A comparison of the passages quoted will make this abundantly evident. These words are inserted by John in the very place, in the series of events, which is occupied by the "loud voice" in the accounts given by the others.

In the light of the passages quoted, we see Jesus spending His last hour on the cross to which His blessed body was fastened by the nails which pierced

His hands and His feet, till the agony of death was passed. We see Him receiving His last drink — and it was vinegar, for nothing less bitter can be given to the Surety of the unjust — and this fitly closes His experience of human cruelty. We hear His last cry and listen to the words which He articulated when that cry was uttered. We hear His last prayer, and though it is addressed to His Father, it arises from the midst of both shame and agony. We can observe His last attitude as He bowed His head and we can appreciate the emblem which it presents of His spirit and of His life. And His last act of obedience followed that token of His meekness for, having bowed His head, He gave up the ghost.

But confining attention to the words "It is finished", I propose to consider them as:

   I. An expression of relief;
  II. An anticipation of satisfying rest;
 III. A shout of triumph;
 IV. A joyful sound to sinners.

I. AN EXPRESSION OF RELIEF

Who can rightly conceive what a relief it was to Jesus, in His perfect human nature, to have passed through all His appointed sufferings? That human nature, perfectly holy, was in a thoroughly abnormal condition when, with all its purity and sensitiveness, it experienced what made the man Christ Jesus a man of sorrows (Isaiah 53:3). As the Surety of the unjust He, when made flesh, occupied such a relation on the one side to God and to His people on the other side, that the most intense sufferings were utterly unavoidable. He, in His mediatorial position, must suffer many things (Matthew 16:21). And in the nature in which He suffered, He was assured of His personal relation, as Jehovah the Son, to the Father who sent Him. His human nature was consciously in union with the divine, as subsisting in the same person with the eternal fulness of the Godhead. And He knew that, though it was in this intimate relation to the Godhead, instead of being security for utter relief from suffering, this only served to make it possible that suffering, such as none other ever endured, would certainly be His experience in the flesh. His eternal Godhead did not fence His human nature against all suffering — it was rather the altar to sustain and sanctify the sacrifice which He was to offer in His people's behalf to God in enduring the full infliction of the curse. He Himself alone would fully know what it was, in the consciousness of His human nature, to have left all suffering behind.

But all His sufferings were left behind, with the exception of His actual experience of death, and His cry is, "It is finished". To His human nature, that never had an experience (except that of the consciousness of perfect love) which was not abnormal, what must the relief have been when what interposed between it and the enjoyment of all that was personally due to Him of blessedness was finally removed!

And how much was finished when His course of suffering came to an end!

1. Relief from being surrounded by sin and enmity

There was all the pain which His holy soul endured from the nearness of the world's corruption and from the virulence of the world's hatred. In the measure of His holiness was the amount of His pain because of the pollution with which He was surrounded. Just think of Him who was "the high and lofty One that inhabiteth eternity, whose name is Holy" (Isaiah 57:15), whose place was on the throne of God for ever: just think of Him in human nature, in the midst of sinful men on the earth — His eyes, His ears, His memory avenues through which there came wave after wave from the ruffled sea of this world's sinfulness and misery to give agony to His soul which was perfect in its love because perfect in its holiness. How could He, but as a man of sorrows, move amidst the corruption and misery of a present evil world? Even if the world were not disposed to persecute Him — even if men did no more than sin in His presence (and by doing so dishonour Him who sent Him, and destroy themselves), He could not, with His perfect love to God and to His neighbour, move in the midst of them without being a sufferer. It was the very love which disposed Him to suffer which made His suffering so intense. He would have suffered less if He had loved less — and yet if He had loved less, He would not have submitted to suffer at all.

But you will say, "Was it not love that disposed Him to suffer, and in the measure of His love therefore He would make light of His suffering?". True, He endured the cross, despising the shame (Hebrews 12:2); but this contempt, while indicating the triumph of His love over all that would intercept Him from finishing His work, was no evidence of suffering being light in His experience. And besides all He had to observe in the conduct of the world around Him, He contemplated the sins which He bore; and though associating these with His loved ones accounts for His having meekly borne the burden of them when the Lord laid them upon Him, that very association occasioned unspeakable anguish to His soul. "This is the sin of My beloved ones, which I can bear only at the cost of being made a curse for them," we might suppose

Him to say. "This is all I have from them. They, My beloved ones, bring on Me all this shame and agony." O what pain it must have given to Him, to have before His pure mind the dishonour to God involved in *their* iniquities, and the madness by which, moved by hatred to Him, they had brought upon themselves the fearful curse of which He had so awful an experience.

And He experienced the malignant hostility of the world in direct assaults upon Himself. His having human nature was taken by men as an opportunity of expressing their enmity in oppressing and afflicting Him. Their persecution of Him began early; and during all His public ministry, in the face of all His manifestations of His glory in His miracles and of all His unwearied course of doing good, it continued to increase — till at last, when the assaults of the powers of darkness were fiercest and the outpoured wrath of God was most overwhelming, their enmity knew no restraint and burst out in cries for His being crucified. They denied His right to be regarded as the Son of God; they disallowed His Messiahship and charged Him with being an impostor; His miracles they ascribed to aid from hell; in order to His betrayal into the hands of the Romans, they watched all His actions and all His utterances, and when they could find no fault in Him at all, they invented charges against Him — they blasphemed and lied in order that they might murder Him. *There* is human nature at its highest in the person of the Son of God — and *here* it is in its low condition, as fallen, in the persons of His crucifiers. Why will men — for there are many such — stand up for the dignity of human nature as represented by the crucifiers of the Lord of glory, while not caring to discern its dignity as it is represented in the person of Emmanuel? There are those who will apologise for His crucifiers and who care not to be transformed into the likeness of the man Christ Jesus.

But all this is now passed. Never again can He in human nature be treated as before. Never shall that flesh in which the Son of God was manifested be nearer to the hands of sinners than a place in the midst of the throne of God; and expressing His sense of relief, Jesus cries "It is finished".

2. Relief from the assaults of the powers of darkness

It expresses His sense of relief from the assaults of the powers of darkness. How hidden is the presence and how mysterious are the operations on the earth of the army of spirits from hell! But their presence and activity are realities in the consciousness of all Christ's followers, as surely as they were in His own. Who can conceive what it was to Him (with His perfect sensitiveness to all that was spiritual and with His perfect abhorrence of all that was unholy) to have hosts of spirits actually assailing Him, to distract Him with all the perturbation which it was in their power to cause? Their very nearness when made felt was agony; and in the felt weakness of human nature to be in actual conflict with them was an experience of affliction which was unspeakably sore. And from the time of the great conflict in the wilderness on to that of the hour of which He said, "this is your hour, and the power of darkness" (Luke 22:53), though we know not what were the instances and the forms of His experiences of temptation by emissaries from hell, we know that at the close, as at the beginning of His public ministry, He knew what it was to bear the assaults of the power of darkness. But the last battle of the war is over and He expresses His feeling of relief when He cries "It is finished".

3. Relief from suffering the wrath of God

These words express His sense of relief from all He suffered in His experience of the wrath of God. Who can enter into the meaning of His own description of His suffering when, speaking to His Father, He says, "I am poured out like water, and all My bones are out of joint: My heart is like wax; it is melted in the midst of My bowels. My strength is dried up like a potsherd; and My tongue cleaveth to My jaws; and Thou hast brought Me into the dust of death" (Psalm 22:14-15). Of course He knew why it was that He bore the wrath of God — that it was because to Him were imputed the iniquities of the people for whom He was Surety.

O think of Him between His Father and His beloved people having to bear the wrath of Him, as the Judge of all, of whom He said "I and My Father are one" (John 10:30) and tracing all the suffering which the expression of that wrath occasioned to the sins of a people whom He loved from everlasting! But God over all and blessed for ever though He was, there was nothing in all that He was and enjoyed that could interpose between Him, as the Surety of the unjust, and the full endurance of the penalty due to the iniquities which He bore. And though He was the only begotten and eternal Son of God, the love of that relationship never for one moment mitigated the expression of judicial wrath bearing on Him as the just suffering for the unjust. Neither His own divine supremacy, nor the infinite love of the Father to Him as His Son, placed any fence between His consciousness as the man Christ Jesus and the full flood of divine anger. Never more certainly was He Jehovah than when enduring the shame and agony of the cross; never more surely the beloved Son than when the Father's face was hidden from Him and when from His desolate soul came the wail — the saddest ever uttered on the earth — "My God, My God, why hast

Thou forsaken Me?" (Psalm 22:1). But instead of imagining that what He was personally mitigated what He endured officially, look (in the light of His unchanging glory and blessedness) on His awful suffering, as stripped naked He hung upon the tree, His blessed body enduring excruciating pain and His soul submerged in the fiery flood of divine wrath — while the hiding of His Father's face made all thick darkness over Him, and pitiless crucifiers compassed Him and scoffing crowds passed Him by in contempt, staying only to wag their heads and rail on Him as they hastened to their marketing in the city.

How much in Jesus' experience of divine wrath must be utterly unknown to us! But of three things implied in it we may be quite assured. Firstly, He had a perfect appreciation of the awfulness of divine anger. Secondly, He was perfectly assured that it bore on Him as the Surety of the unjust. And, thirdly, He actually came in contact with the flaming fire of the expression of that wrath in all the sensitiveness of His perfect holiness. O how terrible to Him it must have been to be without the light of His Father's face! — to Him who was so dependent on fellowship with His Father for His joy. But all this is now past — and who can conceive what His sense of relief was when He cried with a loud voice, "It is finished".

II. AN ANTICIPATION OF SATISFYING REST

Between Jesus and the actual enjoyment in human nature of the rest awaiting Him in the Father's house, there was yet the act of dying. But His eye looked, as to something very near, to the joy set before Him. On that very day His soul was to be in paradise; and, in continuation of this, there stretched eternally before His view what awaited Him as the Lamb who was slain, in the rest and blessedness and glory of a place in the midst of the throne of God. In an anticipation of this as so near, there was present rest to His human soul. And in all His love, as God, to the nature which He assumed, how could He but be glad that His soul and body were so soon to be raised to a place amidst the glory, and to fellowship in the blessedness of being for ever on the right hand of the Majesty on high (Hebrews 1:3)? Only there could holy human nature, subsisting in the person of the Son of God, find its normal condition and its satisfying rest, and only there could the Word made flesh be content to have for ever the nature which made Him a kinsman to His people, and in which for them He glorified the Father on the earth.

1. Satisfying rest in finishing the appointed work

But there was rest to Him, in His zeal for the Father's glory, in the results of the work which He finished on the cross. "I have glorified Thee on the earth," He says to the Father (John 17:4). O, what rest it was to Him to have this to declare! The glory of Him who sent Him was the great end at which He unerringly aimed in all His work as Surety. He desired, at whatever cost to Himself, to satisfy the justice of Jehovah, as Judge, by rendering a full atonement for sin. He desired to magnify the law of God, as Sovereign, and to make it honourable, and to show forth the glory of the name of Jehovah, as this had never been exhibited before. And, in order to this, He yielded Himself up to be so dealt with by God, that there might come forth through Him an infinite manifestation of all divine glory by the rending of His flesh and the shedding of His blood. He perfectly knew that this grand result was secured; and looking on this, in its vastness and brightness, how satisfying was His rest, as with a loud voice He exclaimed "It is finished".

2. Satisfying rest in the result of His work

And there was satisfying rest to Him in the result of His work as bearing on the people whom He loved. For them His Surety work was undertaken — for them it was begun, with His eye on each one of them and His heart as well. He went on suffering while He obeyed, and obeying while He suffered, till the work was finished. He knew that He had endured till He exhausted the curse due to them. He knew that He had done all that was required to secure to them a right to everlasting life, and that nothing was left undone in His fulfilment of the conditions on which He received from the Father the promise that all Israel should be saved in Him with an everlasting salvation (Isaiah 45:17). All this secured, He was at rest. O, think at what a cost He earned His Sabbath! And think of the love that never looks back regretfully on all the toil through which this rest was reached. O! who but an enemy would grudge to the Son of man a Sabbath on the earth? — a Sabbath of which He would be Lord, that it might to the end of time be a symbol and memorial of the rest on which He entered when, raised from the dead, He received a demonstration from heaven of the acceptance of His work.

III. A SHOUT OF TRIUMPH

The very finishing of the work of Christ, viewed apart from its design and results, was a victory. How much and how many interposed between Him and finishing the work which the Father gave Him to do! He could not therefore say "It is finished" without that utterance being the cry of a victor — a shout of triumph. Though Church and State were both against Him, though all classes in the world and all the legions of hell were active in opposing and harassing Him, never for one moment did He falter or stumble in the work. His love triumphed over every affliction. His faith did not for one moment fail. His meekness remained in perfect calmness, unruffled by any of all the storms of persecution which swept over His consciousness. And perfect in every motive, thought, feeling, word and action He went on step by step, through all His course of suffering, till He finished the work which the Father gave Him to do. Who could thus have triumphed but Himself?

But to some eyes the aspect presented by Jesus, as nailed to the tree, is very unlike that of a conqueror. Have not His enemies succeeded in His betrayal and in His condemnation? Has He not by His Jewish enemies been delivered to the Gentiles? Have they not ordered His crucifixion? Has He not been actually led forth to "the place of a skull" bearing the cross that was soon to bear Him? Has He not actually been nailed to it? Hours have passed and none has come to save Him, and do not His enemies twit Him with being powerless to save Himself? And is He not just about actually to die? He is alone in the conflict and the whole result depends on Him. Of the people there is none with Him (Isaiah 63:3), and if He dies, then surely it would seem as if His cause was defeated, and not victorious. Does it become Him, just before bowing His head and giving up the ghost, to utter a shout of triumph? Yes! Verily, nothing ever became Him better than to announce His victory between His last sip and His last breath.

Ah, but look at Him hanging on the tree, showing every sign of being already dead, His last breath having departed just after He had declared with a loud voice that He had won the victory. Yes, I can bear to look on all that proves Him dead, and to think of strong-limbed and stout-hearted Roman soldiers keeping watch around the cross unheeding and unmoved, and of mocking crowds who pass by the crucified, regarding Him as a malefactor who had received the due reward of His deeds. But I must think of some things else. I am not to forget the darkened sun, the awful shadow cast over the face of the heavens, the quaking earth, the rending of the veil, the open graves, the risen dead. I am not to forget a still more marked display of the power of God on conscience in causing even a Roman centurion to glorify God, saying "Certainly this was a righteous man" (Luke 23:47). Furthermore, I am not to forget the trophy of victory taken from beside His cross, when amidst His weakness, shame and agony in the flesh, His power to save prepared a blaspheming thief in a few minutes for paradise; and that even then He could keep in His grasp the cords of love by which He drew out the hearts of a few trembling mourning women after Him. All these things I remember, and they are no signs of His being defeated. Yea, it is when I place what I have produced out of the record as a counterpoise beside all that unbelief would regard as signs of His defeat; then I have both before me, so that I can use them all as proofs that the Beloved has conquered.

Have enemies seemed to make a show of Him openly on the cross? Does His actual death seem to complete their victory? So let it seem to be to every eye on earth but that of faith. All that seeming of victory on their side was required in order to the reality of victory on His. The seeming and real never more widely differed than here. For it was He who made a show of *them* by means of being crucified in weakness — by shame, agony and death on the cross. His victory over His enemies in being obedient unto death, even the death of the cross, secured a resulting victory — a victory which could only be won by dying. His finishing of His work in death was a victory and it secured a victory. For —

1. Christ destroyed the devil

Through death He destroyed him that had the power of death, that is, the devil (Hebrews 2:14). He has the power of death only as the executioner of the sentence of death. Only death can destroy this power of death. The executioner has the power till his work is done. The death which he executes brings his power to an end. He by thoroughly doing his work utterly destroys his power to do it. Here in the case of Christ was One to whom were imputed the iniquities of a people whom only God can number. On Him the devil brought his power of death to bear. And the more certain I am that his work was thoroughly done, the more persuaded I am that his power has been destroyed and that the countless multitude has been redeemed. To assure me of this I need every indication of weakness, every element of shame, every pang of suffering, every token of death that is associated with Christ crucified in the story of the Gospel.

2. Christ triumphed over sin

He in His death triumphed over sin. He made a full end of the guilt, exposing to punishment, of the sins of all the people for whom He died. He made a full and final end of all this. His love could not be satisfied without all this for them. And in order to be sure of this, I require everything I can find in the Gospels which proves that He died in weakness, shame and agony — all that is evidence of His having been made a curse (Galatians 3:13). If sin has brought death on Him, it cannot bring death on His people. The more it seemed to triumph in His death, the less possible does it seem to be that it can triumph in theirs. And by enduring an experience of the condemning power of sin, He secured the condemnation to extinction of sin itself in the souls of all for whom He died. He condemned sin in the flesh (Romans 8:3) by enduring the death to which sinners are condemned. By dying for sin once He secured the utter and eternal death of sin. There is no longer aught to interpose between divine omnipotence, acting in the interest both of grace and holiness, and that abominable thing which God hates and which made loathsome the objects of His love; and its destruction is therefore certain, and is a triumph won by Christ through His being made sin and made a curse (2 Corinthians 5:21; Galatians 3:13).

3. Christ triumphed over the world

He won a triumph over the world. But for His death, all the objects of His love would have been left in slavery, under the despotism of a present evil world. He would fain have them free and He well proved how intently His love was set on their emancipation. But having rendered His due to God in dying for His people, He can now look forward, through death, to the power to save to the uttermost which shall be His when He is at the right hand of the Father. And in full view of the triumph of His power in delivering His people from a present evil world, by drawing them to Himself and by preserving them till they pass out of it at last, His shout is in joyful anticipation of triumph when He cries with a loud voice, "It is finished".

4. The death of death in the death of Christ

He knows that in the moment when His spirit is gone out of His body, to it death shall be for ever past, and He knows that His death shall be the death of the death of all His people. Therefore He anticipates a deliverance from death both for Himself and for all the objects of His love. Death, by its seeming triumph over Him, was death to itself. When He lay under its power, He was preparing for a triumph over it. He triumphed over its terrors in yielding Himself to its stroke — and if He lay dead for a season, it was that His might be an eternal life of triumph over it. The glory of this life as it shone on His view, through the rending of His flesh, evoked a shout of triumph as He exclaimed with a loud voice, "It is finished".

5. Christ's victory over the grave

He could bear to think of His body being laid in the grave, after His soul had passed into paradise, for such was His view of His victory over the grave, that

He could not in the near prospect of it but raise a shout of triumph. How much there is in the burial of Christ, as it lies in between His death and His resurrection! It is the demonstration of His death and it is the occasion of His resurrection. It proves that He loved unto the end (John 13:1) and it furnished an opportunity of proving that He is Almighty. For the sealed stone is removed, the grave clothes are laid aside, the bands of death are broken, the tomb of Joseph is empty again, for the Lord is risen indeed. And as surely as He rose, so shall all His ransomed ones rise. His eye passed on from His own resurrection to its fruit in the resurrection of all the bodies of His people; and His eye rested on the glorious prospect of their being, both in soul and body, perfectly like Him and for ever with Him. Can we wonder, then, that love such as His should break forth in a shout of triumph, in view of such a consummation?

IV. A JOYFUL SOUND TO SINNERS

The loud voice of the High Priest on Calvary reminds one of the sound of old over the burnt-offerings, when the trumpets were blown by the priests in the tabernacle, and afterwards in the temple. And what good news — what glad tidings of great joy — do the words "It is finished" convey!

1. The work of redemption is completed

These words convey the joyful news that the great work of redemption is completed. This work was entrusted to, and undertaken by, Christ alone. There was of the people none with Him (Isaiah 63:3). And as He alone began it, so from His hand alone it received its finish. Emmanuel did it all. Any other hand would mar it. But His hand alone touched it and He leaves the mark of perfectness on every part of it. All the obedience, though rendered in human nature, was the obedience of Emmanuel. All the suffering, though endured in the flesh, was the suffering of the person who is Jehovah the Son. Infinitely meritorious therefore is the Surety righteousness of Christ. The justice of God is infinitely well pleased with His blood as an atonement for the sins of His people, and a sweet smelling savour shall His sacrifice ever yield unto God. The law has been magnified by the obedience of Him who is its Lord, who for a season obeyed it as a Servant. Christ was persuaded of the acceptance of His atoning work by God. In this assurance He exclaimed "It is finished". And gloriously God has declared His acceptance of the work. Each attribute, glorified on the cross, was in the lustre of its manifestation there, at the grave

84

to sanction resurrection work and to shine benignly on resurrection work. Jesus died to the glory of the Father and by the glory of the Father He was raised from the dead. And the High Priest has gone into the holiest with the accepted sacrifice. And the joyful sound of the golden bells (Exodus 28:33-35) — the good news of the Gospel — tells us that He lives and has power with God. And God calls you to His mercy seat, through the rent veil of Emmanuel's flesh, to present yourself as a sinner on the blood that made atonement, as a suppliant for a free and full and final forgiveness of all your sins. Only Christ, only His blood, only His Word — only Christ as the way to God, only His blood as the ground of your pardon and acceptance, only His Word as your warrant for coming as you are and for expecting that redemption in Christ shall be yours. Such is the glad peal that reaches you in the loud cry from the cross.

2. The everlasting covenant is sealed

These words tell you that the everlasting covenant is sealed and that, if you come to Christ, you will obtain on the ground of His finished work a right to all its blessings. The New Testament is in His blood and it, with all it contains, shall be yours, if by faith you receive Christ and His blood as freely offered in the Gospel — and God Himself, as the God of all grace, shall be yours to dispense to you the provision of the covenant graciously, wisely and effectively.

3. Christ secures His people's victory over their enemies

These words tell you that you can find in Christ a right to victory over every enemy. His shout of triumph is an everlasting sound, passing through the Gospel trumpet, telling you that His victory shall be yours in Him if you flee to Him for refuge. O what gladness this should bring to the heart of the oppressed! who can bring nothing but unworthiness before God, and who cannot but as feeble cowards face the enemy in the day of battle. Christ tells you that the victory has been won by the great battle in which He, as the Captain of Salvation, stood all alone against sin, Satan, the world, death and the grave. These all are already conquered. You will be a victor at the outset if you come to Jesus. And though there may be a conflict after this, it is with enemies who cannot take away your life, though they may harass and scare you; while He shall secure to you benefit, even from your wounds, and crown all your experience of His grace with the calm of eternal rest and with the glory and the gladness of eternal triumph.

PRACTICAL APPLICATION

1. How few there are who will stop to listen to this cry from the cross! It continues still to be uttered with a loud voice through the trumpet of the Gospel. You cannot contrive how to escape from hearing it. You have already heard it and your memory preserves it. And you cannot, therefore, escape from it by refusing your earnest attention, or by ceasing to read your Bible, or by absenting yourself from the house of God. Christ crucified is near and His cry is kept up. Memory long ago anticipated the discovery of how to preserve sounds and give them forth again after long intervals; and you cannot at any time escape from yourself. You will carry much of the Gospel in your memory even to hell if you enter it at last, and I know nothing that can more augment your misery there than remembered Gospel truths.

What, then, are you to make of this text? Some of you are so occupied with the things of the world that you grudge a moment of your life to the doctrine of the cross. You go through the wearying, wasting toil of your wonted round of business; or you toil for pleasure till your head is dizzied and your heart is stone. You have neither eye nor ear for Christ because you have no heart for Him; and you pass Him by unheeded, afraid that He may take something from you of what you are so eager to give wholly to the world. Others are averse to look towards the cross or listen to the voice that tells, from out of its shame and agony, that the work of redemption is finished, because they think they have a righteousness of their own which makes them independent of that which was wrought out by Jesus.

Among those who passed by the cross when Jesus was hanging on it and who acted the part of mockers towards Him, there may have been some hurrying to prepare for temple service, as surely as there were some who were hastening to market. These were equally disposed to pass by the glorious sufferer and not to see or hear what might wean them from their idol. And besides these, there may have been some, not intent either on marketing or worship, who were so far away from all that was divine and scriptural through the power of unbelief that, in the scene on Calvary, there was nothing that would for a moment arrest them in their pursuit of pleasure — and nothing even to cause a conscious feeling of any kind towards Him who was lifted up on the tree.

And there are these classes still among the despisers of Christ crucified — the jaded worldlings, the religious toilers and the frivolous pleasure-seekers. In one thing, at least, all these agree — they care not to see the beauty, or to reach the righteousness, or to taste the love of Christ crucified, by the word of His

86

mouth being applied to them with power. Such are some of you, in whichever of the classes of despisers you may be found. But thus saith the Lord, "Behold, ye despisers, and wonder, and perish" (Acts 13:41). And this also He saith, "How long, ye simple ones, will ye love simplicity? and the scorners delight in their scorning, and fools hate knowledge? Turn you at My reproof: behold, I will pour out My Spirit unto you, I will make known My words unto you" (Proverbs 1:22-23).

2. Each one of you all must either receive the words of Christ in the text as true and act accordingly, or reject them, as if they were untrue and act accordingly. From this alternative there is no escape. You must first regard what He speaks about as important ere you will care to believe that what He says regarding it is true. He must be to you the only resort left to you as a sinner. His name must be to you the only one under heaven whereby you must be saved (Acts 4:12). Persuaded that you have been a transgressor from the womb, that the curse of the broken law rests on you, and that power to treasure up wrath against the day of wrath is the only power that is at work within you, how could you fail to be shut out from all hope apart from Christ and His redeeming work? And to you what, in importance, could compare with your being assured that His work was finished, and, because finished by Him, was sufficient as a ground of acceptance with God for the very chief of sinners? If assured of this, then you would seek to lay all your own righteousness aside, that you might come naked, in excuseless guilt, to be clothed with the righteousness which is of God by faith (Philippians 3:9).

But if you do not thus receive the words of Christ, then you must reject them. If you do not believe what He says, then you make Him a liar. And you do so whatever form your rejection may assume.

(a) You do so who say that you require no righteousness either to be wrought by yourself or as wrought by another. O, think of the earnestness of Christ about that as to which you are so indifferent! You reproach Him for regarding a justifying righteousness as something to finish which He would bear shame and agony and death. You mock His suffering and you dispense with His work — and you treat His words with the contempt which is due to a lie.

(b) And you reject His words as if they were untrue, who are still trying to establish your own tottering righteousness. You refuse to listen to Him when He tells you that the work in which you are foolishly engaged has already been finished by Him — and so well finished that nothing besides is required as a foundation of peace with God.

(c) You too reject His words, who are persuaded that apart from Christ crucified there is no hope for you — but refuse to cast yourselves in faith as sinners on Him and on His finished work. You cannot refuse to trust all your eternal interests on that righteousness which He finished, without saying that He has left unfinished His work, which is your only resource.

O, friend, have done with casting dishonour on Him and doing harm to yourself, by refusing to yield to His call when He says "Come unto me, all ye that labour and are heavy laden, and I will give you rest" (Matthew 11:28).

3. Let all whose eye is on Christ crucified, as the one object of their faith, more habitually remember, more heartily cherish, and seek more powerfully to be affected by the words of Christ in the text. Friends, you need to be more under the power of these words in order that there may be more mortifying of your pride of heart. It is this cry of Christ's from the cross that will prove to be the death yet of your legal spirit when applied by the Spirit who can renew as well as impress. If you are a friend of the Crucified One, you will be enemies to all that would spoil Him of His glory. And you need to remember these words when you find no other resource apart from His finished work to which you can repair.

Friends, if these words are true, why should you be afraid? Stand on the work which Emmanuel finished. What besides can you desire as a ground on which to ask the blessing of acceptance with God, on which to claim an interest in all the fulness of the covenant of grace and from which to rise, on the wings of desire and hope, towards the brightness of an eternal triumph over every enemy and of the full enjoyment of God Himself for ever? And you need to be more habitually under the power of these words, in order to a deeper sense of what you owe to Him who uttered them on the cross, that your love may become more fervent, your heart more contrite, your prayers more trustful, your songs more hearty, your service more self-denying, and yourselves more Christ-like.

Redemption and Eternal Inheritance through the Mediator

For this cause He is the Mediator of the New Testament,
that, by means of death, for the redemption of the transgressions
that were under the first Testament, they which are called might receive the
promise of eternal inheritance.

HEBREWS 9:15

In the eighth chapter of Hebrews, the covenant made with Israel, when the Lord took them by the hand to lead them out of the land of Egypt, is contrasted with the everlasting covenant according to which God reserves the salvation of the objects of His love for His own rich grace and almighty hand. True, there was to Israel, under the administration of the national covenant, a revelation of the covenant of grace as well as an exhibition of the terms and terrors of the covenant of works. True, also, those who were believers under that administration found Christ in the types of the ceremonial law and, trusting in Him who was to come, could enjoy somewhat of a child's liberty even under the yoke of the covenant made with their fathers. But the more prominent peculiarity of that administration was the pressure of the law of works; and to all under it who were unbelievers it was in its entirety a yoke of bondage.

But in this chapter, when the two dispensations are compared, it is to mark the difference between the shadow of good things to come and the good things themselves (verse 9). This difference is a marked one as surely as the other. The law was given by Moses as a law of works and as a law of types; but grace and truth came by Jesus Christ — grace in opposition to works and truth in opposition to types. The former is the difference marked in the preceding chapter: the latter that which is brought out in this chapter.

"The first covenant had also ordinances of divine service, and a worldly sanctuary" (verse 1). But both the ordinances and the sanctuary were typical. They were not intended to be final. They were but shadows cast by the coming substance. The tabernacle pointed to the human nature of Christ, which was both temple and sacrifice; and the whole priestly service was but typical of how He who is the Truth executed in human nature His office as the High Priest after the order of Melchisedec (Hebrews 5:6). Apart from Him and His sacrifice of Himself, there was no satisfaction to divine justice or to the human conscience in the many offerings of the ceremonial service. There was a certain efficacy attached to the blood shed and sprinkled according to the law of Moses, but only in so far as it removed such uncleanness as shut one out from the service and privilege of the worldly sanctuary. Only the blood of Christ avails to remove all that interposes between a sinner and the favour of God; and, when applied, to purge the conscience from dead works. And if, to any extent, efficacy is ascribed to "the blood of bulls, and of goats, and the ashes of an heifer sprinkling the unclean", how much more must it be true that the blood of Christ (into which, from His eternal Godhead, infinite merit was infused) must effect the design for which it was shed (verses 11-15).

The words "For this cause" evidently point to the declared efficacy of His priestly action, "He is the Mediator of the New Testament" (verse 15). But this is not the terminus even of this branch of the line of thought. It is not the efficacy of His Priesthood which accounts for His being the Mediator of the New Testament. That accounts rather for His being the Mediator to a certain effect, which is indicated in the words which follow. His priestly action being effective, then there is a "redemption of the transgressions that were under the First Testament"; and this being so, then all who are called may receive the promise of eternal inheritance.

This text presents to us Christ as the Mediator of the New Testament. It ascribes to His death a great redemption, and it tells of a gracious result thereby secured to all which are called. The Mediator, the redemption, the promise — The Mediator redeeming by His death and thus securing the promise of eternal inheritance to all which are called. These are the three points to which the Lord by this text calls our attention:

I. The Mediator of the New Testament;
II. Redemption;
III. The gracious result of the great redemption.

I. THE MEDIATOR OF THE NEW TESTAMENT

1. Christ as the Head of the covenant of grace

Christ has hitherto been usually and properly called the Head of the covenant of grace. He shall continue to be so called by those who have not wearied of the theology of the covenants. But in these days some have become so "broad" that they cannot find room in what was a large place to our fathers. The great apostle of the Gentiles, with the spirit of inspiration to guide him, could not state the doctrines of grace without references, frequent and minute, to the two covenants; but these, forsooth, are wiser. All who were most distinguished as theologians followed the same method as Paul's — and it certainly does seem as if no other course were either wise or dutiful — and yet these refuse their guidance. The fathers, who were eminent for godliness, became so by feeding on the doctrine of the covenants; but this manna is light bread to these. They must be free to adopt their own methods — to be rid of all that is traditional and exact. They are thinkers, forsooth, and they must be free to follow their own bias that they may appear to be original — although their favourable opinion of themselves is the only thing in which many of them are ever likely to be singular. But it is not liberty to think much — to think and to feed — that these desiderate; but liberty not to think definitely — to think and to speculate — not liberty to think according to the mind of God, but liberty to think according as they please.

2. Christ as Mediator of the New Testament

Christ is Mediator of the New Testament. The word rendered "testament" might be rendered "covenant" here, as it is in many other passages. True, the idea of a covenant passes into that of a testament or will in the next verse; and that of Mediator into that of testator — but the transition must not be anticipated. The transition, when it does take place, is easy. According to the covenant, all the inheritance is from the will, the gracious and sovereign will of God; but what God designed for His people is not secure to them, except

91

through the death of Him who is the Covenant Head. What comes to one, according to a testament, is due to the kindly exercise of the testator's will and is secured to the legatee only by the testator's death. And the transition is easy from the idea of Christ as Mediator to that of Christ as testator. If Christ was appointed Mediator, it was with a view to securing a right to the inheritance for His people by His death. The inheritance was in His hands for them and he was willing to die that it might be secured to them; and ascribing to Him, as He is divine, the same sovereignty of love as we ascribe to Him who sent Him, we may trace the legacy secured by His death to His will.

3. Christ as Surety of the New Testament

But Christ, the Head, is called the Surety as well as Mediator of the New Testament. He is the Surety, and must be so, because He is the Head. For, as the representative of the people whom the Father gave Him, He was bound to render all that was due by them and to endure all that was due to them. Neither can He be the Head without being the Mediator of the New Testament; for as such He occupied a position between men and God, and between God and men. He is between men and God in order, in their behalf, to render unto God what He claims from them as obedience and to suffer what was awarded to them as punishment for their sins. And He is between God and men, in order that through Him the provision of God's love may flow to them — that through Him God may deal graciously with them and that they may, through Him, deal hopefully with God.

4. The mediation of Christ

No one can be Mediator except on two conditions:

(a) He must be appointed by God; and yet apart from Himself Jehovah, the Triune, can find none who can execute the office. It would not be befitting, even if it were possible, to appoint one who was not divine; for God must show Himself to be all-sufficient in the fulfilment of His great purpose. All the more must this be true in His way of accomplishing the ends of a scheme of grace. Only a divine agent can or may effect what is required of the Mediator of the covenant of grace.

(b) The Mediator must occupy a position between God and men. Only *there* can mediation work be done.

These two conditions are met by the mediation of Christ.

Christ is a divine person. He is the Word in whom God is fully expressed, and through whom come forth all relevations of His will and glory and all exercises of His power in the fulfilment of His purposes. In perfect consistency with Jehovah's independence, a divine person may mediate; and He who is the Word is the person who, in accordance with the eternal and necessary inter-relations of the divine persons, most fitly mediates. And He is the Son. But He is not to employ His power as Son with the Father in behalf of men, without regard to the interests of God's moral government. He, at the cost of dying, is to maintain the authority and honour of the divine law and lay in divine blood the basis of all gracious action bearing upon sinners. Being the Son, He can do this. His infinite greatness, as the Son, can secure the sufficiency of His atoning work. And on that glory, in the person of the Beloved Son, must our eye rest if we would know how bountifully God can give, and what the love is from which salvation flows. What a Son! What a Father! What a gift is such a Son from such a Father! And what a channel the death of the Son is for the love of Jehovah to flow through on its way to sinners who deserved to die!

And the divine person who is the Son is in a mediational position. This could not be unless He became the man Christ Jesus, while continuing to be all He ever was as the eternal Son of God. It is true He did Mediator's work before His incarnation. Through Him the grace of God flowed out to men; and through Him also believers drew nigh to God in Old Testament times. But the basis of all this, in the view of God in bestowing and in the eye of faith in receiving, was in the incarnation and death of Christ. This all was present to the mind of God, and was presented to and realised by the faith of the saints. He was the Lamb slain from the foundation of the world (Revelation 13:8) before the eye of God, in all His counsels bearing on the salvation of His people on the earth. In that light which comes from the eye, which is as a flame of fire (Revelation 1:14), the Mediator ever presented in His person the divine and human natures, being the eternal Son of God and the brother of the seed of Abraham at once. He could therefore always mediate to the effect of being security to God for all that was due by His people, and of conveying from God to them all that had been promised to Him for them.

And the mediation ceases not with His death. It is true that His servitude ended then, but His mediation still continues. He was serving as incarnate only till His redeeming work was finished. That was the first part of His mediatorial undertaking. But He is no longer a servant. His place as Mediator now is not on the earth in the form of a servant. He is now in human nature on the Throne; and there it is that now He is acting the part of Mediator. He is a High Priest there, presenting before God His accepted sacrifice; and on the ground of it making intercession. And He is exercising His power as Prince in fulfilling, by the ministration of the Spirit, all gracious divine purposes bearing on the people whom He bought by His blood.

He is alive to administer His own Testament. There is no testator like Him in this respect. When other testators die, their will is of force; but others who survive them must be the executors. But Jesus Christ is the executor of His own Testament, which became of force when He died. Is it not well that He shall see of the travail of His soul, and be satisfied with all He secured for the objects of His love being applied to them (Isaiah 53:11)? He shall see His seed, for He can make it certain that all His redeemed shall be quickened by His Spirit and made one with Himself. The pleasure of the Lord, bearing on all His covenant people, shall prosper in His hand. It is delightful to the love of Christ to have the power of an endless life — to use in the salvation of those whom He reconciled by His death. And it ought to be sweet to you, believer, to think of this. How often is your right to what He has bequeathed challenged? And how often are you unable hopefully to plead your cause? But when you are at your wit's end and you have no more to say in defence of your claim, you may repair to Him who is the covenant given to the people (Isaiah 49:8), to take hold of His glorious person and thus have the Head; to claim His precious blood and thus have all the fulfilment of the conditions; to rest on His infinite fulness of grace and thus have all the provision of the covenant. Come, even as you are, for has He not said, "Him that cometh to Me I will in no wise cast out" (John 6:37)? You will find the covenant in Him. You embrace it all in embracing Him, and you pass the challenge, which struck you dumb, on to Him who knows how to make short work of answering it. For if you put your trust in Him, the challenge is no longer of your right to take but of His right to give. O, hear Him say, "I am He that liveth, and was dead; and, behold, I am alive for evermore, Amen; and have the keys of hell and of death" (Revelation 1:18). Think you, cannot He make it sure that all His legatees have the full benefit of all that was bequeathed to them by the bounty of His love and secured to them by the blood of His cross?

II. REDEMPTION

The Mediator's great achievement was the redemption of the transgressions that were under the First Testament. This redemption He effected by means of death. Now, this calls us to consider:

1. What is meant by the transgressions which were under the First Testament?

2. Why had Christ, as Mediator of the New Testament, to effect the redemption of these transgressions?

3. How did Christ effect this redemption?

1. What is meant by the transgressions that were under the First Testament?

Any breach of the law of God is a transgression. It is a guilty act, for it exposes the person who committed it to the endurance of the appointed penalty. Sin shall not be unpunished. There was, there is, there shall be, no sin committed which shall not be punished. Every pardoned sin was punished on the cross, and all unpardoned sins shall be punished in hell. Sinner, seek to realise this!

But you may feel as if there was a restriction here that allowed you no opportunity of looking hopefully on the doctrine of the text. You ask: "Are not the transgressions referred to only those which were committed in the days of old?" True, there is a special reference to these, but such a reference as only helps to open more widely the door of hope to you. The main thing is to show that there was nothing in these days of old by which sin could be taken away, notwithstanding of all the blood-shedding and blood-sprinkling of the tabernacle and the temple. The law of works, then, only served to make sin abound, and the laboured ritual of the law of types left it to abide. Sin abounded and abode under the First Testament. There was nothing to put it away. All transgressions remained under that Testament. And, sinner, is it not so as to your transgressions? They are exposed and condemned by the law of works, under which you are; and they must remain, notwithstanding all that can be done by you or for you, till Christ takes your case in hand. And as of old, the law of works entered that the offence might abound. Was this not the effect of the coming of the commandment to some of you? And the sin remained, and it abounded, so long as you remained away from Christ. But Christ met all the transgressions that were under the First Testament, which were chargeable against those for whom He was Surety; and He can meet all yours as well. The efficacy of His death went back over all *their* past, it can go over all *yours* also — and is all available to this effect for you if you come to the Redeemer.

2. Why had Christ, as Mediator of the New Testament, to effect the redemption of these transgressions?

The answer is, because He was the Surety of the unjust who were condemned to die. He, in their nature, took the place of their Surety under the law; and in that position He could not be without their sins being imputed to Him. It was with a view to bearing — and to bearing away — their sins that He was their substitute. He must satisfy the justice of God for all their transgressions. This necessity arose because of antecedent exercises of love. There was a purpose to save the guilty — there was the provision of a Lamb to bear their sins. That Lamb having come, He must secure the redemption of their sins in the only possible way. That is the burden willingly borne by Him who is both the Lamb and the Son of God.

But it may be asked — Would we not more fitly think of the redemption of sinners than of the redemption of sins as the result of the Mediator's work? But may we not think of their sins as the debts of the people? He bought the bonds by paying the debts. He could do with these bonds what it pleased Him — and what it pleased Him to do was to nail them to His cross. Sometimes among men old debts are bought up in order that the buyer may sue those by whom they are due. But this is not Christ's way of redeeming transgressions. He bought the transgressors themselves by paying all that was due by them and, having done this, He nailed to the cross the handwriting that was against them (Colossians 2:14), and by the power of His life He secures to them the benefit.

3. How did Christ effect this redemption?

By means of death the Mediator thus effected the redemption. There was no other way of it. "Without shedding of blood there is no remission" (Hebrews 9:22). Death, instead of making an end of Him, made an end of sin. "Sin bringeth forth death" (James 1:15). The birth of its progeny is not the end of sin; but the ending of death is the ending of the sin that brought it forth. Death found in Christ one who could make an end of it. The curse of the broken law was exhausted in His dying; and there remained no more death to which guilt could expose. Therefore the guilt perished in a fully accomplished death. Sin was thus made an end of.

Into the humiliation and obedience and shame and agony and dying of the Mediator there came infinite merit from the dignity of His eternal Godhead, so that the law was magnified by His obedience, justice fully satisfied by His suffering, the name of God glorified in His judicial dealing with the man that was His fellow, and a channel opened up through which the rich and holy grace of the covenant may be conveyed by the Holy Ghost to poor sinners on the earth.

III. THE GRACIOUS RESULT OF THE GREAT REDEMPTION

The gracious result of the great redemption was that they which are called might receive the promise of eternal inheritance. Who? and What? must be asked in considering this. Who? — they which are called. What do they receive? — the promise of eternal inheritance.

1. Who receive the promise?

Who receive the promise? They which are called. They only, not all. It was not the end of Christ's dying that any should receive the promise except those who are called. They only who are effectually called by the Spirit, not all who are outwardly called by the Word. Many are called in that way, while but few are chosen (Matthew 22:14). Those only receive the promise to whom the call of the Gospel has been made effectual by the gracious operation of the Holy Ghost. This effectual call was an arresting one, for the Lord took hold of them by a word spoken with power to their conscience. It was an arousing call, and broke up the sleep of the years of their ignorance. It was an alarming call, for the terrors of the Lord took hold of them. It was an abasing call, for they were brought down from one high place after another, till at last, utterly crippled, they could no longer attempt to rise. It was an attracting call, for to their quickened souls the Gospel was so applied that they went forth unto Him who suffered without the camp (Hebrews 13:13). As Zacchaeus was called, so were these. Christ and they met. They received Him into their heart, and He received them into His fellowship. They became one spirit with Him. His righteousness was put upon them and His Spirit was put within them. A covenant God acknowledged them as His people, and the Father adopted them as His children; and then and thus they received an interest in the promise of eternal inheritance.

2. What promise do God's people receive?

They receive the promise of eternal inheritance. In the receiving of the promise there are two steps — the receiving of an interest in the grace of the promise, and the receiving of all the enjoyment implied in the fulfilment of it — attaining a right to and obtaining possession of eternal inheritance. A right the called already have: the possession they shall have hereafter.

A right to the eternal inheritance they cannot but have. They have been called into the fellowship of the Son Jesus Christ. One with Him as the Head of the everlasting covenant, His blood which sealed that covenant is placed to their account. On the ground of that blood (by the shedding of which the conditions of the covenant were perfectly fulfilled) they have a right to all that God promised to Christ for His redeemed. And not only is a right to the eternal inheritance in glory theirs, but to all the grace required in order to prepare them for it and to bring them to the full enjoyment of it. All this is theirs who have been called into the fellowship of the Son Jesus Christ.

And to all the called this promise shall in due time be fulfilled. It is the promise of eternal inheritance. They are heirs because they are sons. They are joint-heirs with Christ, for on the selfsame ground on which He has the inheritance for them, they have the inheritance in Him. And they shall be together, He and they, in the enjoyment. Is heaven the inheritance? That is the place in which the inheritance shall be enjoyed, rather than the inheritance itself. God Himself is their inheritance. To possess the eternal inheritance is fully to know, love, enjoy and serve Him. O, think of what He was to them, as the God of all grace, in order to bring them all holy into His house above! And think of what He, who is the God of all glory, shall be to them as the fountain of their blessedness for evermore! When He called them, it was to His eternal glory. And it is the cause of His glory, as it is the purpose of His heart and the promise of His mouth, to bring them into the full possession of the inheritance which awaits them there.

PRACTICAL APPLICATION

1. I ask you all: "Are you such sinners in your own eyes today that you can have no hope apart from the provision unfolded — the Saviour revealed — in the text?" Apart from Him who is the Mediator of the New Testament, how hopeless must your case be! If He could not redeem but by means of death — His own death on the tree — how can you dispense with Him? You cannot undertake to do and live what He could only do by dying. You are shut up by sin to dying. And *your* dying will perpetuate your sin, as surely as your sin will perpetuate your dying. Only He could make an end of sin and death together. In your experience, if you are not in Him, both sin and death will abide for ever.

2. How anxious you ought to be, therefore, for being effectually called to Christ, that you might find in Him redemption through His blood, the forgiveness of sins, according to the riches of divine grace. Don't refuse to realise your need of this, for you do urgently need it and you must die for ever if you are left without it. And why hide any of your empty vessels when there

is enough in the stores of grace to fill them all? O! cry to Jesus, who proved Himself to be the Christ, by baptizing with the Holy Ghost. He can call you out of the very grave, the deepest and the darkest; from out of the horrible pit and the miry clay He can raise you; from the strong grasp of hell He can deliver you; from the utmost ends of the earth He can draw you. O be not dumb before Him who has all that power, while you are needy, while He is Jesus, and while His power is the might of saving grace!

3. I would like to say a word to the heirs of the promise. In the Lord's presence I charge you with being too little taken up with your inheritance, too ready to distrust Him who secured it for you, too unthankful for the grace that made you to differ, and too ready to be content without the lively exercise of the hope that enters within the veil (Hebrews 6:19). But with all this guilt, repair to the blood to increase your debt to pardoning mercy. Let this always be your way of dealing with any debt to justice you incur by sinning: come and incur a fresh debt to divine mercy for the removal of it. One debt is removed by incurring another. And be dependent on covenant grace for keeping you more watchful, more hopeful and more grateful in the time to come.

4. Are there some of you who think it very unlikely that you can have received the promise of eternal inheritance? Why is this your opinion? Is it because of what you remember of guilt in the past? If so, I would be far from counselling you to ignore that past and by doing so make it easier for you to hope. Conscience must not be thus rudely treated and charges of guilt must not get the go by. Repair, I would rather say, to the blood that sealed the new covenant, and confess your guilt to God, who is gracious and ready to forgive, and again find your way through divine blood to the riches of divine grace. Then will God speak peace again to your heart, and the Valley of Achor, where the sin was disposed of, will be to you a door of hope (Hosea 2:15) through which to look forward to the eternal inheritance. Is it because of what you feel that you are afraid of not being an heir? Is your trouble from without? It so, do not stumble because of this. All who are heirs must pass through great tribulation (Revelation 7:14) to the inheritance; and if you escaped tribulation, it could be only by avoiding the way to the kingdom. Is it from within that your trouble comes? If so, neither stumble because of this. You are needy and find little trace of aught but sin in your soul or in your service. There are some things to which you hesitate to give a name, but there are many things of which you are quite certain that they are not the things which accompany salvation. You cannot therefore venture to conclude that you are among the called who have the promise of eternal inheritance. Yea, sometimes you have the trouble from

without and that from within at once. You are like the vessel in which Paul was, when in the place where two seas met. "Deep calleth into deep" (Psalm 42:7). But, friend, many a king's child has his fits of crying because of pain; and sometimes princes have been in such a plight that they had not a crumb of bread to eat. But you will get over all your poverty and sorrow yet, if you use your need as a reason for keeping near to Him in whom all fulness dwells (Colossians 1:19). It is blessed want that urges you to cry to Him. It is blessed trial that makes you more dependent on His smile. It is blessed weakness that makes you lean more on His strength. It is blessed hunger that makes earnest your cry for bread. It is blessed patience that waits for the Son from heaven, even Jesus who delivered from the wrath to come (1 Thessalonians 1:10).

The preaching of Christ Crucified

We preach Christ crucified.

1 CORINTHIANS 1:23

Verse 18 reads: "The preaching of the cross is to them that perish foolishness" — not because of any defect in the preaching, but because of their own self-conceit and unbelief. Regarding it as foolishness and weakness they derive from it no advantage whatever. But the same preaching is to those who are called, the power of God, all His omnipotence being pledged to save them through Christ crucified. And as it is to no defect in the doctrine of the cross that we are to trace the death of those who perish, so neither must we ascribe the salvation of those who believe to any difference there was, by nature, between them and those to whom the Gospel was "a savour of death". The ruin of the one class is to be traced to their own pride and unbelief, and the salvation of the other to the grace of God.

This double result of the preaching of the cross is to the praise of Him of whom are all things (Romans 11:36). He thus triumphs over the wisdom of the wise and brings to nothing the understanding of the prudent (verse 19). He allowed the wisdom of the world to run its course for generations and the result was the thick darkness of utter ignorance of God. And He allowed those to perish who "by wisdom knew not God", in order to its being made manifest that true light and life can come from Himself alone. And only to His sovereign grace must be ascribed the salvation of those who receive the Gospel, for they are saved, merely because "it pleased God by the foolishness of preaching to save them that believe" (verse 21).

The Jews (whose nation rejected Jesus the Messiah, and the rules of whose church persecuted Him to death) being indisposed to yield to His claims and anxious to justify their unbelief— "require a sign" (verse 22) — some proof, by miracle, of Jesus of Nazareth being the Son and the Anointed of God. "And the Greeks" — enamoured of their learning and prone to continue engaged in profitless speculation — "seek after wisdom" such as their minds can appreciate and their hearts can approve. But in the Gospel there was nothing to gratify either of these. A risen Christ, through His servants, was preaching Christ crucified. And thus the sign of the prophet Jonas was given to men, and no sign besides; and the only wisdom presented to their attention was that which came before them in "the foolishness of preaching". But the Apostle resolved, in all simplicity, to preach Christ crucified, though to the Jews such preaching was a stumbling-block — a thing to give them offence — and to the Greeks, with their affectation of superior wisdom, it was foolishness. But when the Spirit of God interposes in conversion, they which are called are put into connection with all the resources of covenant grace, enter into the security furnished by Jehovah's scheme of salvation, and have begun an acquaintance with its manifold wisdom, and thus to them is "Christ the power of God, and the wisdom of God".

This text requires us to consider the great theme of the Gospel — Christ crucified. This theme is quite outside of the sphere with which the wisdom of this world is conversant. Those who are in there, doing their narrow thinking and enjoying their vain and fleeting pleasures, are prone to think that their little circle encloses all that is wise and estimable — and they are quite disposed to regard as pitiful the lot of those who have no fellowship with themselves. Especially prone are they so to think of those whose study is the doctrine of the cross, for they appear to them to be men of cramped minds and of starved hearts, because they hold aloof both from their speculations and from their enjoyments. To worldly people, the theme to which the godly engrossingly apply their thinking seems uninteresting and narrow, and hidden under a haze which they have no desire to penetrate. But theirs is the narrow range of thought, who, in all their thinking, never enter the sphere of the divine and the eternal. It would ill become the bat to twit the eagle with being unable to enjoy the dark hole in which, during daylight, it finds its resting-place. It is still more ludicrously unbefitting that one, who knows only the wisdom of this world, should despise the man who turns from all that earth can yield to Christ crucified, "the power of God and the wisdom of God". The theme, which he has turned aside from all else to contemplate, is infinite in its wonderfulness and eternal in the gain it yields to all who study it in faith.

I cannot have any true acquaintance with Christ crucified without His wondrous person as Emmanuel being before me. I must consider His commission as Saviour as He is sealed by the fulness of the Holy Ghost, in order to the fulfilment of the divine purpose of grace. All He is and all He has, and all He has done for sinners I must trace up to God and back to eternity when I think of Christ crucified. I must trace on to His incarnation all the providence of God from the beginning, according to His eternal purpose; while His own life in the flesh, back to His birth, must be thought of when I am looking to its close on the cross. And I cannot think of Christ as actually crucified without my mind following the revelation of Him, given in the days of old, back to the first promise which was given in Eden.

Nor can my mind rest on His cross without rising to His crown and, following Him through His burial, resurrection, ascension, reception and enthronement, resting its gaze on the glory and power which are His as He is seated at the right hand of the Majesty in the heavens (Hebrews 8:1). Nor can I think of the power of that life without following the operation of it out from the throne to all the saving benefits which it secures to all for whom He died. And I cannot look on the face of the crucified One with the eye of faith without having the glory of God (as it shines from that face) before me as an infinite and eternal object of contemplation. Nor can I think of the issues of His death and life without passing into eternity and contemplating that everlasting life which those who were ransomed by Christ crucified shall be enjoying in the Father's house. Is there not expanse enough within a theme of such import and suggestions? The mind furthest from being cramped is that of him who desires to glory only in the cross of the Lord Jesus Christ (Galatians 6:14).

But let us more specifically inquire what the words "We preach Christ crucified" imply.

I. We preach Christ crucified to sinners;
II. We preach Christ who was crucified;
III. We preach peace to sinners through the blood of Christ's cross;
IV. Sinners must be told of the saving power of Christ's life as well as of the atoning merit of His death;
V. We preach the love of God to sinners;
VI. We show forth the glory of the name of God.

I. WE PREACH CHRIST CRUCIFIED TO SINNERS

Only to sinners can one preach on such a theme, and only to sinners within the ends of the earth. What have any, who are not sinners, to do with Christ crucified?

He who preaches must be consciously a sinner — yea, the chief sinner in the congregation — ere he can preach aright on such a theme as this. And he must aim at producing a sense of sin in the minds of those to whom he preaches. Without conviction of sin, they will treat with contempt the Christ whom he desires to commend and the salvation which He has secured by the blood of His cross, for "they that be whole need not a physician, but they that are sick" (Matthew 9:12). He must therefore follow in his preaching the divine example of bringing in the law, that the offence might abound (Romans 5:20). Preaching void of this is not accredited by any scriptural example and can never be productive of any good results.

The law must be preached from a heart that trembles before the Word of God — a heart to which the word of condemnation is a burden and that yearns with pity over, and travails in fervent desire for the salvation of, those who are perishing. And why should the preacher ignore the guilt and misery and helplessness of the sinners whom he addresses? He is preaching Christ crucified and he is preaching Him at the command of God. He may well bear to look on the sinner's state when he is presenting to him such a One as He is whom it is his work to preach. He can meet every crime, every want, every ailment and all the impotence of every sinner to whom the Gospel comes. If you came with a skilful physician to the bedside of a poor creature who, covered with "wounds, and bruises, and putrifying sores", was fast dying there, would you not desire to uncover all his ailments that the physician might come in contact with them? And you would do so in kindness and you would do this in hope, because of the presence of one who had skill to cure. To strip the invalid of all that covered his sores, if you were alone, you would regard as cruelty. But with the physician beside you, such work would be kindly.

The command of God leaves no alternative but to preach Christ crucified to every sinner who may have an opportunity of hearing the Gospel, for His orders are "Go ye into all the world, and preach the Gospel to every creature" (Mark 16:15) — to Jew and Gentile, to male and female, to rich and poor, to young and old, to those who have never heard the Gospel before and to those who have long been hardening under it, to the most ignorant as well as to the most enlightened, to those within the Church and to those outside, to the most obdurate as well as to the most impressible, to the most openly ungodly as well as to those who have most of a form of godliness (2 Timothy 3:5), to the bitter persecutor as well as to him who seems to be a friend. To all without exception, therefore, and to all as sinners, Christ crucified must be preached.

"But there are saints, as well as sinners, on the earth," it may be said, and it may be asked, "Is not Christ crucified to be preached to them?" True, there are saints as well as sinners on the earth, but there is no saint here who is not a sinner, though there are many millions of sinners who are not saints. There are those who call themselves saints and who, in hearing the preaching of Christ crucified, take the place that accords with that name and listen to the Gospel as if it were not addressed to them, and thus spend unprofited their season of opportunity. And there are, besides, some who think that their faith has raised them out of the category of sinners, and who, therefore, think that they have had enough to do already with the preaching of the cross and that their absorbing anxiety and labour now must be directed towards making others like themselves. To these the preaching of Christ is a matter of no concern, so far as their own interests are concerned. But not such were the saints of Scripture. Not such was Job or David or Isaiah. And not such was the great apostle of the Gentiles who, on the eve of passing into eternal glory, exclaimed, "O, wretched man that I am! who shall deliver me from the body of this death?" (Romans 7:24) and who expresses, at the close of his life, the ground of his hope for eternity in the words, "This is a faithful saying, and worthy of all acceptation, that Christ Jesus came into the world to save sinners; of whom I am chief" (1 Timothy 1:15).

II. WE PREACH CHRIST WHO WAS CRUCIFIED

When we preach Christ crucified, we preach Him who was crucified. He is preached by those who are His ambassadors, as the person whom God has appointed and sealed to be the Saviour of lost sinners. As such, the preaching of these presents Him to their hearers. He, and He alone, is exhibited as the Saviour whom God has provided. And He must be preached in His personal fitness, as Emmanuel, to execute the great work wherewith He was entrusted. If He were God only, then He could not act the part of a Surety in behalf of the unjust; for, if only divine, He could neither obey nor suffer in their behalf. If He were man only, then how could he effect the redemption of sinners? for there could be no sufficient merit in any work of His as Surety. But He is God manifest in the flesh. Being made flesh, He is the kinsman of the people whom He has engaged to redeem and He can, as their Surety, take their place under the law, to bear their sin and to endure its penalty and, by His obedience, to meet the claims of the law as a covenant of works. And being the Word made flesh, He was able, in human nature, to sustain the weight of expressed divine wrath and so to fulfil all the requirements of the law as to magnify it and make it honourable.

O, what a person this is! O, what is it to hold such a One in the arms of faith? What is it to follow the goings of such a One on His way to the cross? What ravishment a view of His glory, amidst the shame of His cross, gives to him who, by the eye of faith, beholds Emmanuel on the tree! O with what holy reverence, with what humble ecstacy, ought Christ — Emmanuel, the Messiah — to be preached! How dependent ought he who preaches Him to be on the grace of the Comforter, whose work it is to glorify Christ, to receive of His and to show this to His disciples! Is He not "fairer than the children of men" (Psalm 45:2)? Is He not "the standard-bearer among ten thousand" (Song 5:10, marginal reading)? Is He not "altogether lovely" (Song 5:16)? Ought it not to be as a foretaste of heaven to be preaching Him anywhere within the ends of the earth? And will it not be so in the measure in which His glory is discovered and His love constrains?

And this wondrous person is the Christ. God has anointed Him with the fulness of the Holy Ghost. This is the wondrous seal of His appointment to redeem and to save. When one thinks of Him as Emmanuel, how complete, under the light of His personal glory, seems the work which He finished on the cross! And when I realise Him as having the Holy Ghost in all the plenitude [fulness] of His grace and omnipotence in order to fulfil the end for which He was crucified, by the operation of His power, how certain does it appear that He shall see the fruit of the travail of His soul till He shall be satisfied (Isaiah 53:11)? What a light is projected from the cross by His person and His unction! — back on the action of the God of Salvation in the generations of the past; and forward on the providence in which He shall be fulfilling the purposes of His grace till time shall be no more.

III. WE PREACH PEACE TO SINNERS THROUGH THE BLOOD OF CHRIST'S CROSS

We preach Christ crucified and, in doing so, we preach peace to sinners through the blood of His cross. We do so because He, in the work finished on the cross, laid the one foundation on which divine mercy (to the praise of all the divine name) may bestow the blessing of peace on a sinner. O what a blessing is peace with God to a sinner condemned to die! He has been convicted of being a death-deserving sinner; the sentence of eternal death lies upon Him; the face of "God the Judge of all" is set against him; and for him, apart from the sovereign exercise of divine mercy, there is no way of escape from everlasting woe. But that mercy cannot be extended to him except in a way that will secure honour to the law of God, satisfaction to the justice of God, and glory to the name of God. And how can all this be secured? The sinner himself can do nothing to meet the law's claims, for he has no strength, but power to transgress; and the demands of divine justice he himself can only meet by yielding up his whole person, in order to an experience of eternal dying. But Christ crucified has done and suffered all that was required in order to a free and full exercise of divine mercy for such as shall be to the praise of the divine glory. He, as representing all who shall be saved, gave to the law an obedience by which it was magnified, and gave to justice an atonement for sin which was infinitely precious; and He gave an opportunity to God of so dealing with Him — and through Him with sinners — as admits of an infinite display of the glory of all His name.

In preaching Christ crucified there is presented to the sinner this one ground on which he is called to take his stand before the free and infinite mercy of God to receive — without money and without price (Isaiah 55:1) — the blessing of everlasting peace with God. O what would the preaching of Christ crucified be if, with a heart travailing under the sense of an unpardoned sinner's condition and with fervent desire for his escape from the wrath to come, one saw in the light of the doctrine of the cross how God is just in justifying a sinner who becomes the righteousness of God in Christ; if one was persuaded of the infinite bounty of divine mercy and its perfect opportunity of being expressed in the pardon of a sinner for the sake of Christ crucified; and if one had the authority of the command of the Lord to "preach the Gospel to every creature" impressed upon his conscience!

But let us not imagine that in preaching Christ crucified a general amnesty is proclaimed to all who hear the Gospel, and that the mere proclamation of the Gospel of peace suffices to set men free from condemnation. There are not a few who feel and act as if this were all that was required in order to their being at peace with God. Instead of this being so, there are none whose doom shall be more awful than that of those who, having heard the Gospel, received not Christ Himself as therein revealed and offered. It is Christ crucified that is preached when peace through His blood is preached, and not apart from

Himself can the peace which He procured possibly be found. Him "God hath set forth to be a propitiation through faith in His blood" (Romans 3:25); and only as you reach Him in faith and trust in His blood as the one ground of your acceptance before God can peace be yours. Hope because of a general amnesty, as the imaginary result of the Gospel being preached, must end in the everlasting confusion of all who shall continue to the end to cherish it.

But in the preaching of Christ crucified peace (as the gift of divine love, on the ground of the work finished on the cross, and according to the call and promise of God) is in and with Christ crucified, presented and offered to every sinner who hears the Gospel — whatever, besides being a sinner he may be, if only he is a child of Adam within the utmost ends of the earth.

IV. SINNERS MUST BE TOLD OF THE SAVING POWER OF CHRIST'S LIFE

When Christ crucified is preached, sinners must be told of the saving power of His life, as well as of the atoning merit of His death. The preacher must follow the action of God bearing on His Anointed. There was a necessity for His resurrection and ascension constituted by His death on the tree. All He was and all He did demanded His being exalted in human nature to His place as the eternal Son in the midst of the throne of God. For this, because He was crucified, He intercedes: "Father, glorify Thou Me with Thine own self with the glory which I had with Thee before the world was" (John 17:5). This intercession was answered by the Father, and on the record of His responsive action we rise in faith from the cross to the throne of Messiah.

They who preach Christ crucified must be careful to direct the eyes of sinners upwards, from His humiliation to His glory. There are two reasons why they ought to do so. Firstly, because they have to tell poor, sin-sick sinners of His power as a Saviour, as He is now exalted at the right hand of God. And secondly, because they have to tell them of His power as a Judge, who shall yet appear "in flaming fire taking vengeance on them that know not God, and that obey not the Gospel of our Lord Jesus Christ" (2 Thessalonians 1:8). And if they know and love Christ crucified, they cannot but desire to rise to His reward in glory for His death in shame, and to the power which can make the earth the scene of His gracious triumphs in the salvation of the lost.

Let sinners be told that Christ who was crucified is now exalted a Prince and Saviour. Let them be told that all authority and power which He has as a

Prince He exercises as Saviour, and that a complete salvation — beginning in conversion and ending in glory — is the outcome of His life on high. Let them be told that He could not be Christ crucified as the High Priest making atonement, without appearing before God with the blood, which was accepted as a ransom in order to make intercession; that as an Advocate, He has unlimited power with God in behalf of all for whom He pleads; and that all who hear the Gospel are called to receive Him as High Priest, both as an Atoner and as an Intercessor; and that He into whose hands they are called to deliver up their case is able to save to the uttermost all who come unto God through Him (Hebrews 7:25). Let them be told, also, that as Prince and Saviour He can give "repentance and remission of sins" (Luke 24:47); that He can turn sinners "from darkness to light, and from the power of Satan unto God" (Acts 26:18), thus bringing them in among the people whom the God of salvation claims as His own — and giving them, in a free and full remission of all their sins, a blessing in the train of which shall reach them all the good things of the everlasting covenant of grace. Let them hear, too, that He lives to preserve the poor and needy from all deceit and violence (Psalm 72:13-14) and to cleanse them from all their defilement, till He has brought them without spot or blemish into the rest and blessedness and glory of the Father's house. Again and again, and yet again, to the close of one's preaching, let them hear of Christ's right and power and willingness to do all this for every sinner, whatever and wherever he is, who comes to Him in reponse to the call of God in the Gospel.

V. WE PREACH THE LOVE OF GOD TO SINNERS

They who truly preach Christ crucified preach the love of God to sinners. If they preach Him as the Lamb, they must preach Him as the Son and as the gift of God. They cannot think of Him who, being the Son, is the gift of God, without tracing up this unspeakable gift to the infinite and sovereign love of Jehovah the Father. Infinite and sovereign must be that love ere the preaching of it can be good news to sinners. If it were not infinite because divine, and if the expression of it were not as surely infinite as the love itself, how could a sinner expect such an outflow from it as he requires in a free and full and everlasting salvation? And if any reason apart from the sovereign will of God could be assigned for God's loving sinners, then no one who knows himself as guilty and loathsome could ever hope that divine love could be expressed in His salvation.

It is only because His love is sovereign that one can possibly have hope in God. There are not a few who are prone to rise aflame against the doctrine of the sovereignty of divine love when it is presented in a plain statement before them, who in secret before God just hope because they believed that God had before His mind, in loving sinners, no worthiness or inducement on their part to draw forth His love. He loved them just because so it seemed good in His sight. And the grand proof of this is given in the cross, and cannot therefore be ignored in the preaching of Christ crucified. How can the Son's being Christ crucified be otherwise accounted for? What could there be in the necessary relation between God and His Son, and between Him and sinners on the earth, to account for such a manifestation of His love? If His Son is Christ crucified in order that the objects of His love might be saved, surely they must have been, in the judgment of God, hell-deserving sinners and must owe it to the unaccountable will of God, as Sovereign, that they are loved and saved. Such a ransom would not have been exacted or provided by God if there was aught connected with them to commend them to His favour.

These two grand truths regarding the love of God must be preached to sinners — that the love of God to sinners is infinite, and that it is sovereign. That it is both appears in the commendation given of it in His Son being His Christ, and in His Christ being crucified. And there can be therefore no reason why anyone disposed to approach that love, through the way opened up on the cross, should shrink back from it because of aught that he brings, in his case as a sinner, whatever and whoever he be.

Let the preacher tell each sinner whom He addresses, that nothing can interpose in Christ the way between him and the infinite and sovereign, and therefore free, love of God; that this love with outstretched arms awaits him with an embrace; and that no fear is more groundless than that of not being received with infinite gladness when he comes. Let him again and again be reminded of how God's love to sinners has been commended. Let his attention be directed to the infinite majesty and glory of Him who loved; to the relation in which He stands to Him whom He sent to redeem His loved ones by His blood; to all the shame and agony, culminating in the cross, which His Son endured as the Surety of the unjust; to all that is involved in the purpose of salvation which through Christ crucified He fulfils; to all the antecedents of that love in the salvation of sinners during the ages of the past, and to the assurance of a welcome given by God in declaring that He hateth putting away (Malachi 2:16).

If anyone says that, as the love of God commended in the gift and death of Christ is sovereign love to a people whom He elected to everlasting life, he therefore has no encouragement to appeal to or approach it, let him be told that he has nothing to do with the secret purpose of God, as a rule of faith; that the elect are by nature children of wrath even as others; that it is as love to sinners that His love to them was revealed and commended; that no way of expressing His love to them could be suitable except as it bore on them as sinners; that the love of the cross, expressed in blood-shedding, must have been love to sinners; and that this is the aspect which the love commended through Christ crucified presents to us. Let him be told that God is to be known according as He revealed His name, and not according as He has formed His purpose; and that therefore His love, having been expressed as love to sinners, each one who hears the Gospel may be assured that God will act according to His name towards every sinner who comes to Him through Christ crucified, as preached to every creature.

And let sinners be told that the love of God will not be satisfied without the coming sinner being made one spirit with the Lord and being, by adoption, made a child of God and a temple of the Holy Ghost; that His love will continue to be expressed during all the believer's life on earth in preserving, teaching, sanctifying and comforting him till He has led him to, and prepared him for, everlasting glory; and that, once at home in the Father's house, he shall never cease perfectly to enjoy the expression of God's love and to be filled with the palace-feast which it has prepared for the children of the King.

And let all who hear the Gospel be assured that to remain faithless towards Christ crucified is to refuse the embrace of divine love and to flee from the God of all grace to the misery of eternal dying.

VI. WE SHOW FORTH THE GLORY OF THE NAME OF GOD

They who preach Christ crucified are bound to show forth, in so far as by the Spirit's help this is possible, the glory of the name of God. For, as nowhere else, that glory appears in the face of Christ crucified. He came to reveal the Father and in the measure in which He Himself appears is the Father also seen. "He that hath seen Me," He says, "hath seen the Father" (John 14:9). Every evidence given by Jesus of His disposition towards sinners is to faith an opening through which to look into the heart of Him who sent Him. All His meekness in suffering was an evidence of the divine supremacy. Every miracle He performed was a proof of divine omnipotence. And all His purity was the light of Jehovah's holiness shining through the flesh in which the Son of God was manifested. And He revealed the Father in His doctrine, in which He referred to His sovereignty and to His love, to His scheme of salvation, to His relations to His people, and to the aspect which he presents to all transgressors of His law and to all despisers of His Messiah and His salvation.

1. The glory of Christ's work as Redeemer

But it is through His work as Redeemer that the divine glory specially shines forth. Divine wisdom is displayed in the adaptation of Christ's person, as incarnate, to the position which He was to occupy and to the work which He was under engagement to fulfil; this divine wisdom shines forth gloriously in the adaptation of His work to the claims of God on the one hand and to the state of the sinner on the other. How such an adaptation could be secured was the highest problem ever solved by the wisdom of God. Through Christ crucified appears the glory of divine wisdom as in no other manifestation of Himself which God has given. Only as one enters into the manifold wisdom of God in the great scheme of redemption is he a child of light. All from whom the wonders of grace are hidden have no other wisdom than that which is foolishness with God.

2. The glory of divine truth

And let the praise of divine truth be proclaimed as it appears in the fulfilment of purpose and promise in the cross of Christ. From all eternity Christ gave promise to the Father of finishing in an accursed death the work of redeeming the people whom the Father gave Him. How glorious is His truth as it appears in His death on the tree! And the promise of the Son's coming and dying as Messiah the Redeemer was given four thousand years before — and yet with all the unworthiness of the objects of His love fully before His mind, with His eye, all these years, resting with infinite love and delight on the person of His only begotten Son, and while all the shame and agony of His life and death in the flesh was in the Father's view, He gave Him in the fulness of time even unto death. O what a display of divine truth is this! How excuseless is unbelief towards such a One! What risk can be run, in suspending oneself over eternity, with the whole weight of a seemingly desperate case, on the truth of a word which the mouth of the Lord hath spoken?

3. The glory of divine justice

And in the cross of Christ, as nowhere else, appears the glory of divine justice. For there we see Jehovah's fellow and His beloved Son, as the Surety of a people whom God loved from everlasting, dying an accursed death because the sins of these were imputed to Him! There was, in His favour, no mitigation of the sentence of death. The cup filled with the bitterness of the curse due to the unjust was drunk to its dregs by the Just One — Jehovah in His love of righteousness demanding this as satisfaction for the offences of His chosen people! How inflexible this justice! And if just in the measure in which this is appreciated one cannot but tremble, how sweet, at the same time, is the gladness flowing from the hope which this display of righteousness fosters in the heart of a believing sinner! For, as this stern work of justice was exhausted in the suffering of the Surety, is not a way seen to be opened for the outflow of divine mercy? — the sword that smote in the interest of righteousness opening up the way through which grace can come forth with salvation, and the sinner may approach the mercy-seat.

4. The glory of the holiness of God

And let the preacher tell of the holiness of God, as this is revealed through Christ crucified. It is impossible that God can tolerate sin. Here are the sins of a people whom He loved from everlasting laid upon the man who is His fellow, and against these He comes forth as a consuming fire, and the agony of the "Holy One and the Just" (Acts 3:14) is the result! Thus only can sin be made an end of as a crime. But the design of removing at such cost the guilt of sin is that He by His Spirit coming forth, through divine blood, might be a consuming fire to all the corruption by which His loved ones are defiled! Such a procession, and such a work as follows that procession, form surely the highest display ever given of Jehovah's holiness! O, how lovely is the salvation which is invested with all this beauty of holiness! How worthy of God it is! How infallibly certain it is that it cometh from "the high and lofty One that inhabiteth eternity, whose name is Holy" (Isaiah 57:15).

5. The glory of the love of God

And all this manifestation of glory accompanies the commendation of divine love. Regarding that love, of which the Gospel testifies, nothing can be learned apart from Christ crucified. Only in the cross of Christ appears love to sinners — that singular love of the Holy One. And it there appears — though love to sinners — a true, just and holy love, as well as infinite and free; while all its outflow is directed by infinite wisdom as it bears on those who are its objects.

And through the cross, and through it alone, not only appears the love of God to sinners, but He Himself appears as He is love (1 John 4:16). Who can conceive what God is in His capacity of loving? Who can do this, even with the full light of the doctrine of the cross shining on His name? But He is there, as He is love, for He appears in the light of an infinite display of Himself as such. Yes, He Himself is there in the full glory of His love. O, what a sight is this for the eye of faith! O, what a theme is this for the preacher of Christ crucified! Never throughout eternity can even His saints in glory go beyond beginning to behold the wonders which are unfolded in the relevation of God as He is love. Love to Himself, love to righteousness He was, is, and must for ever be — but that His power to love an object apart from Himself should find its fullest demonstration in the exercise of His saving grace bearing upon sinners is a wonder which should excite the admiration of saints and of angels for ever.

CONCLUDING REMARKS

The text determines what is the preacher's theme. If he who professes to preach ignores the doctrine of the cross, he can have no message from God to sinners. His gospel cannot be "good tidings of great joy", it cannot be "the word of salvation", nor can it be "the Gospel of peace", neither can it be the means of bringing men to deny ungodliness and worldly lusts and to live soberly, righteously, and godly in this present world (Titus 2:12).

In the estimation of many, the Pauline preaching is becoming an antiquated kind of thing which, in an age such as ours, should be quite laid on the shelf as a fossil. And what do they propose to substitute?

Some would have a more unsystematic mode of presenting truth. They would cast the federal [covenant] theology aside, and must have a fresh cast of thought and an altogether new phraseology. And what is this new thing which they have introduced? It is not easy to describe it, for it is neither law nor Gospel — and it is a rare eye that can discern it to be common sense! It is suited neither to saint nor to sinner — and where to find an audience for such preaching, in which neither of these shall be, it is utterly impossible to conjecture.

Others would have intellectual preaching, from which the old story of the cross would be excluded, and nothing supplied either for the heart or for the conscience.

Others still desiderate what they regard as advanced teaching. Of course in their view this crave is a desire for progress — but what really is the thing which they seek? It is to go back from all the positions reached during the religious conflicts of the past, to abandon the whole sphere of vital godliness, to treat with disrespect the divine authority of the Word of God, and to decry as superstition all effort to walk in the fear of the Lord.

Besides all these there are some who are enamoured of what they call practical preaching, by which they mean preaching which is not doctrinal — for they dislike to be made to feel how ignorant they are of the divine scheme of grace. This is preaching which (taking it for granted that all are Christians) deals out its counsels to all indiscriminately; and which, coming down to the everyday cares and anxieties of life, tends to cheer men in their daily toil by comforts which are furnished by reason rather than by Scripture — comforts which never flowed from the fountain of living waters through Christ crucified.

These are the new styles of preaching — and if recent progress is maintained, Pauline preaching will soon cease to be heard from Scottish pulpits.

"We preach Christ crucified." Only in connection with the preaching of Christ crucified will the quickening Spirit come to beget the life which is developed in new obedience. And it is the doctrine of the cross alone, when effectually applied, which can be the motive power under whose impulse a Christian walks in the ways of the Lord.